PHILADELPHIA
USA

PHILADELPHIA
USA

ROBERT H. WILSON

PHOTOGRAPHS BY CHARLES P. MILLS

DESIGN BY RAYMOND A. BALLINGER

PUBLISHED BY CHILTON BOOK COMPANY

SPONSORED BY GIRARD BANK

AN OFFICIAL PHILADELPHIA '76 BICENTENNIAL PUBLICATION

Philadelphia '76, Incorporated is the official agency
for coordinating observance of the 1776 Bicentennial in Philadelphia,
the birthplace of the United States.
The Corporation extends its sincere thanks to
Girard Bank, of Philadelphia, which has sponsored the
publication of this volume as one of its Bicentennial projects.

Typesetting by John C. Meyer & Son, Inc.
Printing by Smith-Edwards-Dunlap Company
Binding by Hallowell and West

Philadelphia, a great modern city, is a metropolis of widely diverse commerce, industry and finance; and it is one of the world's major seaports. A center of education, medicine, law, music, fine arts and religion, it is also a livable city of comfortable homes and convenient transportation. But Philadelphia is best known as a city of history. William Penn granted Philadelphians religious freedom and self-government nearly a century before 1776. Benjamin Franklin, the most famous man in colonial America, lived and worked here. In Philadelphia, independence was declared, the United States of America was born and George Washington served as first President. The attractiveness of twentieth century Philadelphia is the way the old, historic city has been carefully preserved in the midst of the modern as seen in this view from the visitors' center at the top of Penn Mutual Tower on Independence Square.

Philadelphie, grande métropole moderne, est aussi la ville la plus chargée d'histoire des Etats-Unis. L'ancienne cité est soigneusement préservée au coeur de la ville moderne comme on peut en juger par cette vue prise du haut de la tour de la Penn Mutual de l'Independance Square.

Philadelphia, eine moderne Weltstadt, ist historisch gesehen, die bedeutendste Stadt Amerikas. Dieser Blick vom Penn Mutual Tower auf den Independence Square zeigt, dass die von neuen Bauen umgebene Altstadt gut erhalten ist.

Filadelfia, gran metrópoli moderna, es también la ciudad más histórica de los Estados Unidos. La ciudad antigua está cuidadosamente preservada dentro de la nueva, como puede apreciarse en esta vista tomada desde la torre del edificio de la Penn Mutual en Independence Square.

William Penn's Quaker "Experiment"

Philadelphia was founded in 1681 by William Penn, an English Quaker. Penn received a grant of 26,000,000 acres from King Charles II who named the Province "Pennsylvania". For the principal settlement, Penn chose the Biblical name "Philadelphia"—meaning "City of Brotherly Love".

A huge statue of "Billy Penn" at the top of City Hall tower is Philadelphia's best known landmark. By common consent, but not as a matter of law, no building in the city rises higher than the base of the Founder's statue.

The tower statue, erected in 1894, was modeled after one executed a century before in England which was presented to Pennsylvania Hospital by Penn's grandson and now stands in the yard of the hospital at Eighth and Spruce Streets. In the left hand is shown the historic 1701 Charter of Liberties in which Penn granted his colonists religious and political freedom. The original charter is preserved at the American Philosophical Society.

C'est William Penn, le Quaker anglais à qui appartenait toute la province de Pennsylvanie, qui fonda Philadelphie en 1681. Sa statue gigantesque qui surmonte l'Hôtel de Ville en est le monument le plus connu. Une autre statue, plus ancienne celle-là, au Pennsylvania Hospital, le représente tenant à la main sa fameuse Charte des Libertés, rédigée en 1701.

Philadelphia wurde im Jahre 1681 von dem englischen Quäker William Penn gegründet. William Penn war ebenfalls der Gründer der gesamten Provinz von Pennsylvania. Die bekannteste Sehenswürdigkeit der Stadt ist die Statue Penns auf dem Turm des Rathauses. Ein älteres Denkmal auf dem Gelände des Pennsylvania Hospital zeigt Penn mit der historischen Charta der Menschenrechte von 1701.

Filadelfia fue fundada en 1681 por el cuáquero inglés, William Penn, quien fue dueño de la entera provincia de Pensilvania. Una enorme estatua de Penn, situada encima de la torre del Ayuntamiento, es el monumento más conocido de la ciudad. Una estatua más antigua, en el Hospital Pennsylvania, muestra a Penn sujetando en la mano su histórica Carta de Libertades de 1701.

Unlike earlier colonists in Virginia and Massachusetts who struggled to build homes in the wilderness, those who came to Philadelphia in 1681 were purchasers of lots in a well planned community. Before any left Europe, Penn's surveyor had laid out the city in a checkerboard of straight streets and open park spaces.

The original plan is still the design of modern Philadelphia. City Hall stands in the Center Square, which is named for Penn himself. The other four squares still exist, named for Franklin, Washington, David Rittenhouse and James Logan. This is Logan Square, northwest of City Hall.

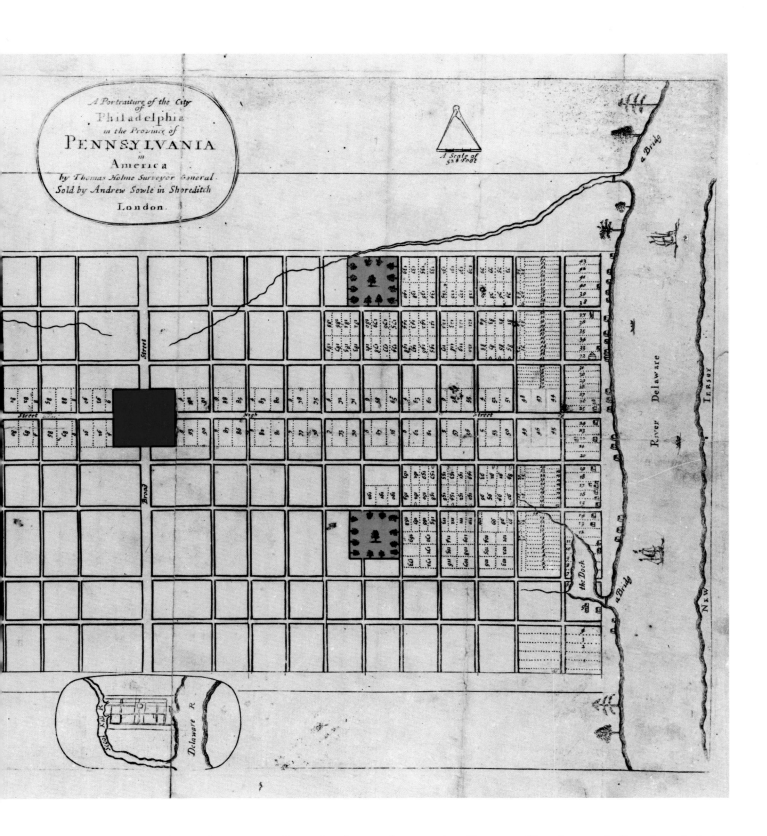

Sur l'ordre de Penn les plans de la future ville furent tracés avant que les premiers colons viennent s'y établir. Les rues et les parcs originaux existent toujours. Voici le Logan Square, situé au nord-ouest de l'Hôtel de Ville.

Penns Landmesser fertigten den Plan für die Stadt Philadelphia an, bevor die ersten Siedler eintrafen. Die ursprünglichen Strassen und Parkanlagen existieren heute noch. Das Bild zeigt Logan Square, nordwestlich vom Rathaus.

El agrimensor de Penn levantó el plano completo de Filadelfia antes de que se poblara la ciudad. Todavía existen los espacios originales de las calles y parques. He aquí Logan Square, al noroeste del Ayuntamiento.

The stately government building begun in 1732 for the Province of Pennsylvania is occasionally called The State House by some Philadelphians, but most of the world now knows it as Independence Hall.

Meeting here in 1751, the Provincial Assembly voted to purchase a 2,000 pound bell for the tower then being added to the building. The year 1751 was a jubilee year—the 50th anniversary of the Charter of Liberties granted by Penn in 1701. A scholarly committeeman delegated to choose an appropriate inscription for the bell turned to the Old Testament Book of Leviticus. Chapter 25, Verse 10, referring to ancient Hebrew tradition of freeing bondmen in jubilee years, begins: "And ye shall hallow the fiftieth year, and proclaim liberty throughout all the land unto all the inhabitants thereof." The concluding words became the first line of the inscription. The second line read: "By order of the Assembly of the Province of Pensylvania for the State House in Philada."

The bell was made in England, arrived in Philadelphia in 1752 and cracked while being tested after a rough ocean crossing. The "Ingenious Work-men", Pass and Stow, recast it; and beginning in 1753, its booming tone was heard throughout Colonial Philadelphia.

Cet édifice majestueux, plus connu maintenant sous le nom de "Independance Hall", fut bâti en 1732 pour abriter l'Assemblée de la Province de Pennsylvanie. La cloche fut commandée en 1751 pour commémorer l'anniversaire de la Charte des Libertés. On y grava la citation biblique: "Vous carillonnerez la sainteté de ce cinquantenaire et la liberté qui règne sur notre pays".

Dieses eindrucksvolle Gebäude wurde im Jahre 1732 als das State House von Pennsylvania errichtet. Heute ist es als Independence Hall bekannt. Die Glocke wurde 1751—zum fünfzigsten Jubiläum von Penns Charta der Menschenrechte—erworben. Das folgende biblische Zitat wurde damals als Inschrift für die Glocke gewählt: "Und Ihr sollt Freiheit für alle Bewohner im Lande verkünden".

Este majestuoso edificio, denominado actualmente Independence Hall, fue construido en 1732 como edificio de la Cámara Legislativa del estado. La campana fue comprada en 1751 con motivo del quincuagésimo aniversario de la Carta de Libertades de Penn. En ese mismo año se escogió la inscripción bíblica que lleva inscrita la campana: "Proclamaréis la libertad en toda la tierra para todos sus habitantes".

In 1698, Old Swedes' Church (Gloria Dei) was built just to the south of Philadelphia by Swedish settlers who had lived along the Delaware for half a century before Penn became Proprietor. This building replaced a log structure which had served both as blockhouse and place of worship.

Penn insisted that his Province be "an Holy Experiment" where all people—not just Quakers—could worship God as they chose. Members of the Swedish church, originally Lutheran, eventually united with the Church of England, and Gloria Dei is now an active Episcopal parish with services every Sunday.

Penn proclama que sa province serait une "sainte expérience" où tous, non pas seulement les Quakers, pourraient adorer Dieu comme ils l'entendraient. Voici Old Swedes' Church (Gloria Dei) construite de 1698 à 1700, juste au sud des limites de la ville. Elle est toujours dédiée au culte et on y célèbre les offices tous les dimanches.

Penn erklärte seine Provinz als "ein heiliges Experiment", in der alle Menschen, nicht nur Quäker, vollständige Glaubensfreiheit geniessen. Das Bild zeigt Old Swedes Church (Gloria Dei), die in den Jahren 1698-1700 erbaut wurde und sich ausserhalb der südlichen Stadtgrenze von Philadelphia befindet. Noch heute werden dort jeden Sonntag Gottesdienste abgehalten.

Penn manifestó que su provincia era un "Experimento Sagrado" donde todo el mundo—no sólo los cuáqueros—podría venerar a Dios como prefiriera. Esta es la iglesia de Old Swedes' (Gloria Dei), edificada en 1698-1700 y situada al sur de los confines de la ciudad de Filadelfia. Esta iglesia aún permanece activa y celebra servicios todos los domingos.

On the second floor of the State House, the Governor's Council Chamber was the executive office of the colonial Province and, later, the early State of Pennsylvania.

Au second étage se trouve la Salle du Conseil du Gouverneur, d'abord siège du gouvernement de la province, puis du nouvel Etat de Pennsylvanie.

Die Beratungskammer des Gouverneurs im ersten Stock des State House war die Verwaltungs—behörde der kolonialen Provinz und später des jungen Staates von Pennsylvania.

En el segundo piso de la State House se encuentra la Cámara de Consejo del Gobernador, que fue el despacho ejecutivo de la provincia colonial y, posteriormente, del nuevo estado de Pensilvania.

The earliest Quaker meeting houses in Philadelphia were eventually replaced by newer and larger structures such as the ample brick Arch Street Meeting near Fourth Street. It was built in 1804 on land which William Penn had originally deeded in 1693 for a burial ground. Every spring, the Philadelphia Yearly Meeting of the Religious Society of Friends is held here.

Of the original meeting houses in Penn's province, the oldest survivor is that of Merion Meeting. It was erected in 1695 by Welsh Quakers who settled on a large tract west of the city. Penn himself once spoke here at a Meeting for Worship in the same plain little room in which services are still held every Sunday, or First Day.

Les premiers temples des Quakers furent remplacés par d'autres plus grands comme celui d'Arch Street qui fut élevé en 1801, tout en brique. Le plus anciens de ces premiers temples est le "Merion Meeting" construit par des Quakers du Pays de Galles établis à l'ouest de la ville.

Die ältesten Gemeindehäuser der Quäker in Philadelphia, wie das Gemeindehaus an der Archstrasse, das im Jahre 1804 erbaut wurde, wurden durch neuere und grössere ersetzt. Das älteste der Originalgebäude ist das Merion Meeting, das 1695 von Quäkern aus Wales gebaut wurde, die sich westlich von Philadelphia niederliessen.

Los templos más antiguos de los cuáqueros en Filadelfia fueron reemplazados por otros más grandes y modernos, tal como el templo de la calle Arch, enorme edificio de ladrillo construido en 1804. El más antiguo de los templos originales es Merion Meeting, edificado en 1695 por los cuáqueros galeses, que poblaron la región occidental de Filadelfia.

Colonists of many different religious groups followed the Quakers to Philadelphia and established houses of worship which still exist in the modern city.

A Jesuit priest built St. Joseph's Church near Fourth and Walnut Streets in 1733 at a time when the laws of Great Britain forbad celebration of Catholic Mass elsewhere in the English world. The church has been rebuilt, but the entry-way from Willings Alley is reminiscent of colonial days.

The Penn family in 1738 sold to Nathan Levy the lot on Spruce Street near Eighth which became the burial ground of Mikveh Israel, the first Jewish congregation. It was not until after the Revolution that the congregation built its first synagogue. Now it plans to build a new one on Independence Mall.

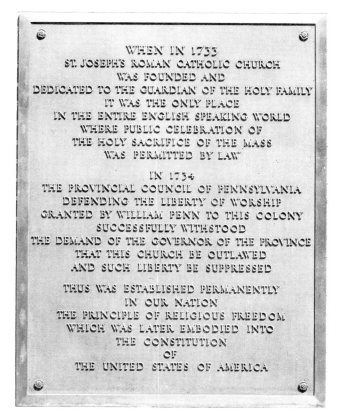

WHEN IN 1733
ST. JOSEPH'S ROMAN CATHOLIC CHURCH
WAS FOUNDED AND
DEDICATED TO THE GUARDIAN OF THE HOLY FAMILY
IT WAS THE ONLY PLACE
IN THE ENTIRE ENGLISH SPEAKING WORLD
WHERE PUBLIC CELEBRATION OF
THE HOLY SACRIFICE OF THE MASS
WAS PERMITTED BY LAW

IN 1734
THE PROVINCIAL COUNCIL OF PENNSYLVANIA
DEFENDING THE LIBERTY OF WORSHIP
GRANTED BY WILLIAM PENN TO THIS COLONY
SUCCESSFULLY WITHSTOOD
THE DEMAND OF THE GOVERNOR OF THE PROVINCE
THAT THIS CHURCH BE OUTLAWED
AND SUCH LIBERTY BE SUPPRESSED

THUS WAS ESTABLISHED PERMANENTLY
IN OUR NATION
THE PRINCIPLE OF RELIGIOUS FREEDOM
WHICH WAS LATER EMBODIED INTO
THE CONSTITUTION
OF
THE UNITED STATES OF AMERICA

Des colons appartenant à de nombreuses autres religions suivirent les Quakers à Philadelphie. En 1738, la famille Penn vendit à la congrégation juive, Mikveh Israel, le terrain destiné à son cimetière. Un Jésuite fit bâtir l'église Saint-Joseph en 1733, alors que la célébration du culte catholique était interdite partout ailleurs dans l'empire britannique.

Kolonisten verschiedener Glaubensbekennung folgten den Quäkern nach Philadelphia. 1738 stellte die Familie Penn den jüdischen Bewohnern der Stadt ein Grundstück zur Verfügung, das zum Friedhof der Gemeinde Mikveh Israel wurde. Ein Jesuitenpater erbaute im Jahre 1733, als die katholische Messe in der ganzen englisch-sprechenden Welt verboten war, die St. Joseph's Church.

Colonos de numerosas creencias religiosas siguieron a los cuáqueros a Filadelfia. En 1738 la familia Penn vendió el terreno que más tarde llegó a ser el cementerio de la congregación judaica, Mikveh Israel. Un sacerdote jesuita erigió la iglesia de Saint Joseph en 1733, año en que se prohibió la celebración de la misa católica en el mundo de habla inglesa.

The Colonial City of Benjamin Franklin

Elfreth's Alley remains much as it was when Philadelphia was the leading city of the thirteen colonies. Near Second and Arch Streets, surrounded by a busy commercial neighborhood, it is still a quiet place of private residences.

In 1723, at the nearby riverfront, Benjamin Franklin first landed in Philadelphia. His *Autobiography* tells how he walked along just such streets as this, a hungry 17-year-old printer looking for work. The statue portraying his arrival stands in front of Franklin Field, the athletic stadium of the University of Pennsylvania.

Five years after his arrival, Franklin began his own printing business. The next year he bought out a one-year-old newspaper and built it into the largest in the colonies. At 27, he began publishing *Poor Richard's Almanack*. He earned a fortune by the time he was 40, and lived to 84— scholar, scientist, diplomat, statesman and Philadelphia's greatest citizen.

Elfreth's Alley, proche de la deuxième rue et d'Arch Street, est à peu près telle qu'elle était en 1723 alors qu'un jeune imprimeur, Benjamin Franklin, arrivait à Philadelphie en quête d'un emploi. Sa statue, commémorant cette arrivée, se trouve au campus de l'Université de Pennsylvanie.

Elfreth's Alley, in der Nähe der Kreuzung der Second Street und der Arch Street, ist heute noch fast in gleichem Zustand wie im Jahre 1723, als der junge Benjamin Franklin in die Stadt kam, um Arbeit als Buchdrucker zu suchen. Zur Erinnerung an seine Ankunft in Philadelphia wurde auf dem Gelände der University of Pennsylvania eine Statue von ihm errichtet.

Elfreth's Alley, callejón situado cerca de las calles Second y Arch conserva casi todas las mismas características de 1723, cuando el joven Benjamín Franklin llegó a buscar trabajo de impresor. En los terrenos de la Universidad de Pensilvania puede verse la estatua que conmemora el día de su llegada a Filadelfia.

William Rittenhouse, one of Penn's early settlers, set up the first paper mill in America in 1690 on the bank of Wissahickon Creek. In 1707 he built this little house nearby, and it is still here although auto traffic now speeds quite close to the door. In this house David Rittenhouse, mathematician and astronomer, was born in 1732. He became a friend of Franklin and was director of the first United States mint. Rittenhouse Square is named for him.

Ces maisons ont appartenu à de grands hommes de Philadelphie. Dans la plus petite, près de Wissahickon Creek, David Rittenhouse, l'astronome, naquit en 1732. L'autre, demeure élégante, fut construite en 1728 par James Logan qui la baptisa "Stenton". Elles sont maintenant la propriété de la Ville.

Diese Häuser gehörten zwei bedeutenden Männern aus Philadelphias Kolonialzeit. Der Astronom David Rittenhouse wurde im Jahre 1732 in dem kleinen Haus in der Nähe des Wissahickon Creek geboren. James Logan baute sein elegantes Haus, das er Stenton nannte, im Jahre 1728. Beide Häuser sind jetzt im Besitz der Stadt Philadelphia.

Estas dos casas pertenecieron a dos grandes hombres de la Filadelfia colonial: David Rittenhouse, astrónomo, nacido en 1732 en una pequeña casa cerca del Wissahickon Creek, y James Logan que en 1728 hizo construir su elegante residencia de Stenton. En la actualidad ambas casas son propiedad de la ciudad de Filadelfia.

One of the largest of Philadelphia's colonial mansions—still in its unaltered form—is Stenton, the fine brick home built by James Logan in 1728. Originally it stood in a wooded, 500 acre tract well north of the city. Its separate back kitchen and its large stone barn are still intact.

James Logan first came to Philadelphia as William Penn's secretary at the age of 25. He became agent and spokesman for the Proprietor and his family in Pennsylvania, an able administrator of public affairs and a successful businessman in his own right. He was in his fifties when he built this lovely house now owned by the city, furnished and maintained by the National Society of the Colonial Dames of America in the Commonwealth of Pennsylvania. Here the scholarly Logan assembled a collection of classical and scientific books which surpassed all the personal or college libraries in colonial America. He left it to the people of Philadelphia.

James Logan vint à Philadelphie à l'âge de 25 ans en qualité de secrétaire de William Penn. Plus tard, homme d'affaires accompli, il devint le mandataire de la famille Penn et l'administrateur de leurs biens en Pennsylvanie. Il avait passé la cinquantaine quand il fit bâtir cette ravissante demeure où il constitua la bibliothèque la plus importante des colonies anglaises d'Amérique.

Als Sekretär William Penns kam der junge James Logan zum ersten Mal nach Philadelphia. Später wirkte er als Verwaltungsbeamter und vertrat die Rechte der Familie Penn in Pennsylvania. Er war auch ein erfolgreicher Geschäftsmann. Mit etwa 50 Jahren liess er dieses schöne Haus bauen, wo er die beste Bibliothek Kolonialamerikas zusammenstellte.

El joven James Logan llegó a Filadelfia por primera vez como secretario de William Penn. Posteriormente fue administrador y portavoz de la familia Penn en Pensilvania, así como también un próspero hombre de negocios. Esta hermosa residencia la hizo edificar cuando tenía alrededor de cincuenta años. En ella fundó la biblioteca más importante de la América colonial.

Gardens, tree-lined streets and hundreds of original colonial homes keep Philadelphia as Penn wanted it: "a greene Country Towne."

Grâce à ses jardins, ses rues bordées d'arbres et ses centaines de maisons d'époque coloniale, le centre de Philadelphie a gardé l'aspect que lui voulait William Penn, celui d'une ville de province verdoyante.

Gärten, von Bäumen umgebene Strassen und hunderte von ursprünglichen Kolonialbauten erhalten Philadelphia so, wie Penn es sich vorgestellt hatte: Als eine grüne Stadt.

Jardines, calles arboladas y cientos de casas de estilo colonial original, conservan a Filadelfia tal como Penn la concibió: "una ciudad provincial, verdosa".

Streets and houses of eighteenth-century Philadelphia help create a unique style of city life for twentieth-century residents.

Les quartiers aux maisons du dix-huitième siècle créent une atmosphère unique pour les habitants de notre époque.

Strassen und Häuser aus dem Philadelphia des 18. Jahrhunderts tragen zum einzigartigen Stil des Stadtlebens der Bürger des 20. Jahrhunderts bei.

Las calles y casas de Filadelfia del siglo dieciocho han creado un estilo único en la vida urbana de sus habitantes del siglo veinte.

The occupants of these tiny houses on Third Street near Pine take pride in maintaining them in the fashion of the year they were built—1771. This is less than a mile from the busiest corner of downtown Philadelphia.

Les propriétaires de ces petites maisons de la 3ème rue, près de Pine Street et à proximité du centre, ont à coeur de leur conserver leur aspect original de la fin du dix-huitième siècle.

Die Bewohner dieser kleinen Häuser in der Third Street in der Nähe der Pine Street sind stolz auf ihre Wohnungen und erhalten sie im Geiste der Zeit, in der sie gebaut wurden (1771).

Los residentes de estas pequeñas casas de la calle Third, cerca de la calle Pine, están muy orgullosos de conservarlas según el estilo de 1771, época en que fueron construidas.

In a home built in 1759 on Spruce Street near Second, the original kitchen with its deep fireplace has been made into an exquisite overnight guest room. Cooking for the present owners of this fine town house is done in a modern kitchen elsewhere in the house.

L'ancienne cuisine de cette maison de Spruce Street, datant de 1759, a été transformée en chambre d'ami.

In einem aus dem Jahre 1759 stammenden Haus in der Spruce Street in der Nähe der Second Street wurde die ursprüngliche Küche in ein geschmackvolles Gastzimmer umgebaut.

En una casa que data del año 1759, situada en la calle Spruce, cerca de la calle Second, se ha transformado la cocina original en un encantador cuarto de huéspedes.

On petition of Philadelphia members of the Church of England, a minister was sent in 1695, and the first Anglican church was built on Second Street near Market. Queen Anne, of England, sent a 1708 silver communion service which is still used on special occasions.

The original church was soon outgrown so in 1727 Christ Church began the large Georgian edifice which is still in service. Still displayed on its east wall, over the Palladian window, is a medallion with the head of King George II who was on the throne when the building was completed.

Christ Church became the fashionable church in early Philadelphia. Its membership included Franklin, Washington and many other historic figures. Seven signers of the Declaration of Independence are buried either in the churchyard itself or in the burial ground which the church established at Fifth and Arch Streets, then the far edge of the city.

Christ Church fut fondée en 1695. L'église originale fut remplacée en 1727 par cet imposant édifice géorgien. On y célèbre toujours les offices, on y utilise toujours le service à communion offert par la Reine Anne et on peut encore y voir le médaillon de George II sur le mur oriental. Sept des signataires de la "Déclaration de l'Indépendance", dont Benjamin Franklin, sont enterrés soit dans le cimetière de l'église soit dans celui situé à l'angle d'Arch Street et de la 5ème rue.

Die 1695 gegründete Christ-Kirche errichtete im Jahre 1727 dieses grosse Gebäude im georgianischen Stil. Es ist heute noch in Benutzung und ein altes Silberservice, ein Geschenk der Königin Anne ist immer noch in Gebrauch. An der Ostwand des Gebäudes sieht man heute noch ein Bildnis von Georg der II, König von England. Sieben Unterzeichner der Unabhängigkeitserklärung wurden im Kirchhof (an der Second Street in der Nähe der Market Street) oder auf dem Friedhof an der Kreuzung der Fifth und Arch Street begraben.

La congregación de Christ Church, fundada en 1695, construyó este gran edificio estilo georgiano en 1727. Esta iglesia todavía celebra servicios religiosos, utiliza aún el juego de plata obsequiado por la Reina Ana, y en su pared oriental ostenta el retrato de Jorge II de Inglaterra. Entre los que firmaron la Declaración de Independencia, siete están sepultados, ya sea en el cementerio de la parroquia (calle Second, cerca de Market), o bien en el que está situado en las calles Fifth y Arch.

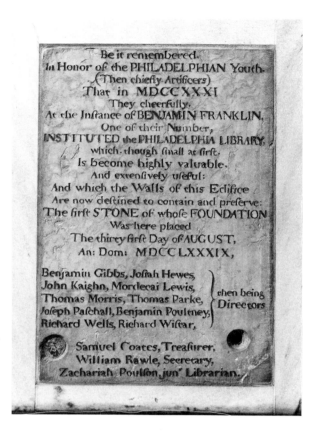

Young Benjamin Franklin persuaded fifty of his friends to form The Library Company of Philadelphia in 1731. It was a club whose members pooled dues to purchase books in England. For half a century the Library rented space, but the year before Franklin died it was able to put up its own building on Fifth Street. Franklin wrote the inscription for the cornerstone and lived to see the building completed in 1789. But he died before the statue of him was erected over the doorway. A William Birch print of 1800 shows the Library as it was then.

The Library Company moved in the 1880s, and its original building was torn down to make room for an office building. Now, that process has been reversed, and the office building has been demolished. On the same spot, and in the same architectural style as Franklin's building, there now stands the Library of the American Philosophical Society.

As for The Library Company of Philadelphia, now nearly 250 years old, it is still thriving. At its present headquarters on Locust Street near Thirteenth, the weather-worn Franklin statue and the cornerstone of the original building are exhibited.

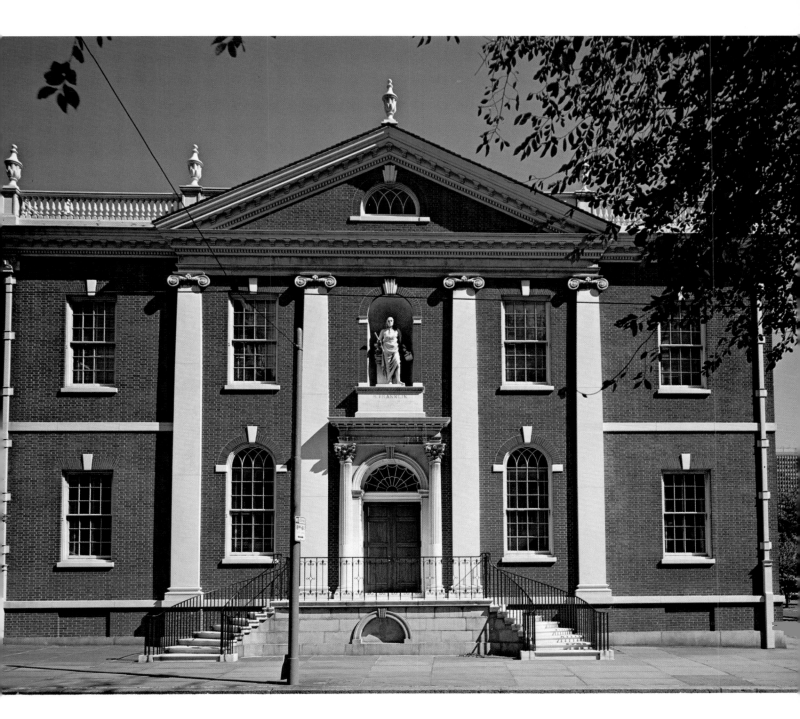

Le jeune Benjamin Franklin fonda en 1731 "The Library Company of Philadelphia" (société d'achat de livres). On détruisit l'immeuble original il y a plus de cent ans mais l'American Philosophical Society en a fait édifier une réplique au même endroit pour abriter sa propre bibliothèque. Quant à la compagnie de Franklin elle prospère toujours deux cent quarante-cinq ans après. A son siège actuel, 1314 Locust Street, elle conserve la première pierre du bâtiment original portant la dédicace écrite par Franklin et la statue de ce dernier qui se trouvait jadis dans une niche au dessus de la porte principale.

Im Jahre 1731 gründete der junge Benjamin Franklin die Library Company of Philadelphia. Das ursprüngliche Gebäude wurde vor hundert Jahren abgerissen, aber die American Philosophical Society baute es an der selben Stelle genau nach. Die jetzt fast 250 Jahre alte Gesellschaft gedeiht heute noch. In ihrem Hauptsitz wird der von Franklin für das ursprüngliche Gebäude beschriftete Grundstein aufbewahrt sowie ein Denkmal Franklins, das in dem alten Gebäude über der Tür angebracht war.

En 1731, el joven Benjamín Franklin organizó la Library Company de Filadelfia. La construcción original fue derribada hace un siglo, pero la American Philosophical Society ha erigido una réplica del edificio en el mismo sitio. La Compañía Franklin se encuentra todavía próspera a pesar de contar con casi más de 250 años. Su sede actual aún conserva la piedra angular del edificio con la inscripción original escrita por Franklin, así como una estatua de éste, colocada a la entrada de la Compañía.

This beautiful room in the present building of Benjamin Franklin's Library Company is named in honor of James Logan, the great Philadelphian who came to America with William Penn and in later life was Franklin's friend and adviser. The Library Company is the custodian of the 2000 volume personal library which Logan gave to Philadelphia.

The view of Independence Hall is from a window of Philosophical Hall, headquarters of the prestigious American Philosophical Society founded by Franklin in 1743. Franklin served as president for twenty years. Among his possessions owned by the Society are the folding library chair from his home and a battery of Leyden jars used in his electrical experiments.

James Logan légua à la Ville sa bibliothèque personnelle comprenant deux mille volumes qui se trouvent maintenant réunis au siège de la "Library Company" où cette très belle pièce porte son nom.

Cette vue d'Independance Hall est prise de l'immeuble de la prestigieuse "American Philosophical Society" fondée également par Franklin en 1743. On peut y voir un certain nombre d'objets lui ayant appartenu, en particulier son fauteuil de bureau et une série de bouteilles de Leyde.

Dieser schöne Raum, heute ein Teil der Franklin Library Company, wurde James Logan zu Ehren benannt. Die grosse Privatbibliothek, die 2000 Bücher umfasst, wurde von Logan zusammengestellt. Diese Büchersammlung, eine Schenkung Logans an die Stadt, befindet sich heute noch in der Library Company.

Dies ist der Blick auf die Independence Hall von dem Hauptsitz der berühmten American Philosophical Society, die von Franklin im Jahre 1743 gegründet wurde. Die Gesellschaft ist im Besitz von mehreren Gegenständen, die Franklin gehörten; unter ihnen befindet sich sein Lesestuhl und eine Elektrobatterie.

Esta hermosa habitación que se encuentra en el edificio actual de la Library Company de Franklin fue nombrada en honor de James Logan. En este edificio todavía se conserva la gran biblioteca personal de 2,000 tomos que Logan coleccionó y donó a la ciudad.

Esta vista de Independence Hall fue tomada desde la oficina de la prestigiosa American Philosophical Society, sociedad filosófica que Franklin fundó en 1743. Dicha sociedad posee muchos de los bienes de Franklin, como ser su silla de biblioteca y una batería eléctrica.

At the request of Thomas Bond, physician member of the Philosophical Society, Franklin raised money to establish Pennsylvania Hospital, the first in the colonies. He was one of the original directors, and when the first building was erected in 1755 at Eighth and Spruce Streets, Franklin was the author of the appealing inscription on the cornerstone near the doorway. The original building is used today for offices.

IN THE YEAR OF CHRIST
1755
GEORGE THE SECOND HAPPILY REIGNING;
(FOR HE SOUGHT THE HAPPINESS OF HIS PEOPLE)
PHILADELPHIA FLOURISHING,
(FOR ITS INHABITANTS WERE PUBLICK-SPIRITED)
THIS BUILDING,
BY THE BOUNTY OF THE GOVERNMENT,
AND OF MANY PRIVATE PERSONS
WAS PIOUSLY FOUNDED,
FOR THE RELIEF OF THE SICK AND MISERABLE.
MAY THE GOD OF MERCIES
BLESS THE UNDERTAKING!

Franklin apporta aussi son concours à la fondation de deux institutions qui existent toujours : le Pennsylvania Hospital et une compagnie d'assurance dont l'emblème (en haut à droite) figure sur les immeubles assurés. Une compagnie concurrente, remontant à 1784, a un arbre pour emblème.

Franklin war der Mitbegründer von zwei Institutionen, die noch heute in Philadelphia bestehen. Es handelt sich um das Pennsylvania Hospital, an der Kreuzung der Eighth und der Spruce Street, und eine Feuerversicherung, deren "Hand-in-Hand"—Wahrzeichen an den von ihr versicherten Gebäuden zu finden ist. Eine weitere, im Jahre 1784 gegründete Versicherungsgesellschaft besteht heute noch. Ihr Wahrzeichen ist ein grüner Baum.

Franklin contribuyó al establecimiento de dos instituciones que todavía prosperan en Filadelfia. Una es el Pennsylvania Hospital en las calles 8 y Spruce. La otra es una compañía de seguros contra incendios, cuya insignia consiste en dos manos enlazadas, y puede verse en la fachada de los edificios asegurados. Una segunda compañía, fundada en 1784, todavía es activa y su insignia de fuego está representada por un árbol verde.

Franklin also helped organize a mutual fire insurance company which is still in business—The Philadelphia Contributionship for the Insurance of Houses from Loss by Fire. Its "Hand-in-Hand" firemark with the date of the company's founding, 1752, is a familiar sight on insured properties. The company now occupies a house on Fourth Street near Walnut built in 1836 to serve both as business office and residence of the clerk.

After The Contributionship stopped insuring houses with shade trees because of greater fire hazard, a second insurance company was formed in 1784 by a group of Philadelphians who described themselves: "Proprietors of Houses who have found it convenient and agreeable to them to have trees planted in the Streets before their Houses." Their company, also still thriving, is The Mutual Assurance Company for Insuring Houses from Loss by Fire. Understandably, its firemark is a spreading green tree.

40

Lemon Hill and Mount Pleasant (below) are country estates of early Philadelphians now owned by the city as part of Fairmount Park.

Lemon Hill was originally the property of Robert Morris, banker, friend of Washington and financier of the Revolution. His mansion was burned during the war. A wealthy merchant later built the present dwelling with the unusual bowed facade which follows the lines of oval-shaped rooms on each of the floors within. He chose the present name of the estate be-cause of the lemon trees Robert Morris had grown in his greenhouse.

Mount Pleasant was built in 1761 on high ground overlooking the Schuylkill. Its occupants included Washington's drill master, Baron von Steuben, and the first Spanish minister to the United States. When he was President and living in Philadelphia, John Adams called Mount Pleasant "the most elegant seat in Pennsylania." The traitor, Benedict Arnold, once purchased the estate as a wedding present for his young Philadelphia bride, but they never lived in it.

Mount Pleasant, ci-dessous, et Lemon Hill, situées dans le Fairmount Park sont deux des propriétés de campagne des premiers Philadelphiens. Elles appartiennent maintenant à la Ville. La première, construite en 1761, était considérée par John Adams comme "la demeure la plus élégante de Pennsylvanie". L'autre fut la résidence de Robert Morris, le banquier qui finança la Révolution.

Lemon Hill und Mount Pleasant (unten) sind zwei von den Landgütern, die den frühen Bewohnern Philadelphias gehörten, und die jetzt als Teil des Fairmount Parks Stadteigentum sind. Lemon Hill war einst das Landgut von Robert Morris, dem Finanzier der Revolution. Mount Pleasant, erbaut 1761, wurde von John Adams als "der eleganteste Landsitz Pennsylvanias" bezeichnet.

Lemon Hill y Mount Pleasant (abajo) son dos de las haciendas de los primeros habitantes de Filadelfia, que han pasado a ser propiedad de dicha ciudad y forman parte del Parque Fairmount. Lemon Hill en una época perteneció a Robert Morris, financiero de la Revolución. Mount Pleasant, edificada en 1761, fue llamada por John Adams "la residencia más elegante de Pensilvania".

One of the best of Philadelphia's country estates of colonial days is Woodford, also in Fairmount Park. A small farm house in William Penn's time, it was substantially enlarged and improved by William Coleman, a judge and friend of Franklin, who acquired it in 1756. Once used as a station house by park police, the house has been beautifully restored and furnished by the Naomi Wood estate as "an illustration of household gear during the colonial years." It is included in park house tours conducted by the Philadelphia Museum of Art.

Woodford, dont la construction remonte à 1756, est une autre propriété située dans le Fairmount Park. Elle a été restaurée et meublée en style colonial grâce au fonds Naomi Wood destiné à cet effet.

Woodford ist ebenfalls ein kolonialer Landsitz in Fairmount Park. Die heutige Villa stammt aus dem Jahre 1756. Die Inneneinrichtung wurde von der Naomi Wood Stiftung zusammengestellt und stellt einen Haushalt aus der Kolonialzeit dar.

Woodford es otra hacienda colonial del Parque Fairmount. La actual mansión, que data de 1756, fue amueblada con los bienes de Naomi Wood como "reflejo de los artículos de uso hogareño de la época colonial".

Franklin and his wife are buried near the Fifth and Arch Streets corner of Christ Church graveyard. The old brick wall has been opened for a short distance so visitors can see the simple stone which is marked exactly as Franklin directed. Often they leave pennies on the grave of "Poor Richard."

The national memorial to Philadelphia's greatest man is the fine seated statue in Franklin Hall of the Franklin Institute. The Institute's building located on Benjamin Franklin Parkway, was partially financed by a trust which Franklin created for the city.

La tombe de Benjamin Franklin et de sa femme se trouve dans le cimetière de la paroisse de Christ Church, presque au coin de la 5ème rue et d'Arch Street. Les touristes y déposent souvent des pièces de monnaie. La belle statue de lui que l'on peut voir au Franklin Institute est un hommage de la nation à ce grand Américain.

Franklins Grab befindet sich auf dem Friedhof der Christ Kirche, an der Kreuzung der Fifth und der Arch Street. Es wird oft mit Kleingeld geschmückt, das von Besuchern gespendet wird, um den "armen Richard" zu ehren. Die Stadt errichtete Benjamin Franklin zu Ehren die schöne sitzende Statue in der Franklin Hall des Franklin Instituts, das an dem Benjamin Franklin Parkway liegt.

La tumba de Franklin se encuentra en el cementerio de la Iglesia de Christ, en las calles Fifth y Arch. A menudo se encuentra cubierta de centavos que los turistas dejan en homenaje "al pobre Richard". El monumento que la ciudad erigió en memoria de Franklin es la excelente estatua que se encuentra en el Franklin Hall del Franklin Institute, institución situada en la Benjamin Franklin Parkway.

City of Independence

Le premier Congrès continental se réunit en 1774 au Carpenters' Hall que venait d'achever la corporation des charpentiers qui y tient encore ses réunions de nos jours. Les délégués y siégèrent du 5 septembre au 26 octobre. Ils se séparèrent alors, non sans avoir décidé d'un autre Congrès pour 1775 ". . . à moins que nous n'obtenions satisfaction à nos doléances".

When political tension brought a call for "a congress of Delegates from all the Colonies" in 1774, it was natural that the meeting should be held in Philadelphia.

A new little hall had just been put up near Fourth and Chestnut Streets by a private trade organization, The Carpenters' Company of the City and County of Philadelphia. It was offered to the delegates and was chosen as the meeting place of the First Continental Congress in preference to the Pennsylvania State House two blocks away. The Congress met from September 5 to October 26, 1774 in this first floor room. Upon adjournment, the delegates resolved that another Congress should meet in 1775 "unless the redress of grievances, which we have desired, be obtained before that time."

Carpenters' Hall was located far back on its lot in order to leave room for other buildings which would provide revenue for the Company. The Carpenters' Company, now consisting of about 90 building executives and architects, still owns the historic building, still maintains it and holds its own meetings there.

Der erste Kontinentalkongress fand im Jahre 1774 in diesem kleinen Gebäude statt, das zu jener Zeit von der Carpenters Firma erbaut wurde. Die Abgeordneten tagten vom 5. September bis zum 26. Oktober und beendeten ihre Sitzung mit dem Plan, einen zweiten Kongress im Jahre 1775 zusammenzurufen: "es sei denn, die Behebung des Übelstandes, die wir verlangen, wird noch vor dieser Zeit eintreten." Die Firma Carpenter ist immer noch der Besitzer des Gebäudes und gebraucht es heute noch für ihre Sitzungen.

En 1774 se reunió el Primer Congreso Continental en esta pequeña sala de sesiones que la Compañía Carpenter en esa época había terminado de construir. Los diputados se reunieron desde el 5 de septiembre hasta el 26 de octubre, y después de proyectar otro congreso para 1775, suspendieron la sesión, "salvo que antes de esa fecha quedaran reparados todos los agravios". La Compañía Carpenter todavía es dueña de esta sala de sesiones donde hasta la fecha celebra sus reuniones.

Within a month after the First Continental Congress adjourned, 28 gentleman members of the Gloucester Fox Hunting Club met in the same building, Carpenters' Hall. They organized themselves into a military unit, The Light Horse of the City of Philadelphia, and offered their services in the approaching conflict with Great Britain. When war came, they served as a reconnaissance force for Washington, were commended by him and eventually became his official escort when he was President.

Since that time, the Troop has served in every time of war and, in colorful uniforms with plumed helmets, has been the escort for United States Presidents on visits to Philadelphia. Officially, the organization is Troop A, First Squadron, 223d Cavalry, Pennsylvania Army Reserve National Guard. Philadelphia calls it The First City Troop.

In November 1974, the Troop celebrated its bicentennial with services at the same colonial church where it first worshipped in 1774—St. Peter's at Fourth and Pine Streets. St. Peter's was built in 1761 and is still maintained by its own congregation to serve an active Episcopal parish.

En 1774, vingt-huit membres d'un club de chasse au renard fondèrent une unité de cavalerie qui combattit sous les ordres de George Washington et qui lui servit de garde à cheval pendant sa présidence. Depuis lors elle escorte tous les Présidents des Etats-Unis en visite officielle à Philadelphie. Depuis sa fondation ses membres assistent au culte à St. Peter's Church (4ème rue et Pine Street) où elle a célébré son bicentenaire en 1974.

Achtundzwanzig Mitglieder eines Fuchs-jagdvereins organisierten 1774 einen berittenen Truppenverband. Sie dienten unter Washington, wurden zu seiner offiziellen Eskorte, als er Präsident war, und seit dieser Zeit begleiten sie die Präsidenten während ihrer Besuche in Philadelphia. Im Jahre 1974 feierte der First City Troop sein zweihundertjähriges Jubiläum mit einem Gottesdienst in der St. Peter's Church, also in derselben Kirche, in der die Truppe im Jahre 1774 zum ersten Mal betete.

Veintiocho socios de un club de caza organizaron, en 1774, una unidad militar de caballería montada. Dicho grupo prestó servicios al General Washington, convirtiéndose en su escolta oficial cuando éste fue elegido Presidente y, desde entonces, ha escoltado a todos los Presidentes en sus visitas a Filadelfia. En 1974 esta unidad (First City Troup) celebró su bicentenario con servicios religiosos en la iglesia de St. Peter —calles Fourth y Pine—en el mismo recinto donde aquella primera tropa había rendido culto en 1774.

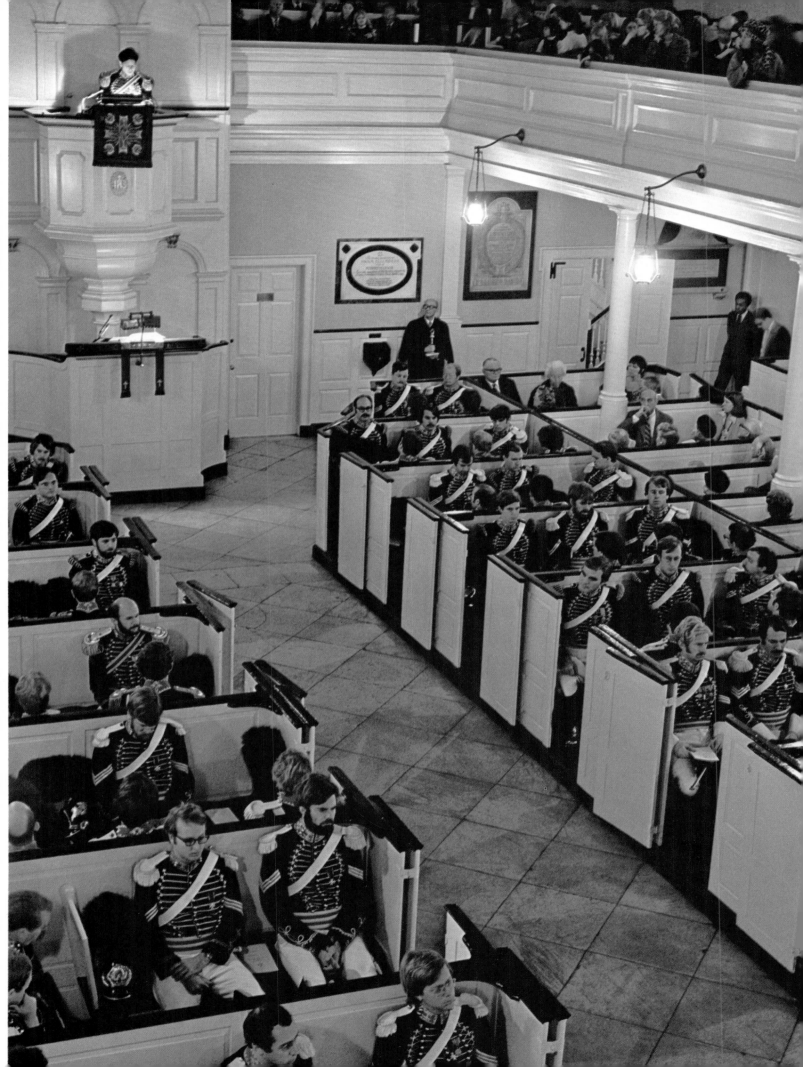

The Long Room on the second floor of the State House was the scene of many festive occasions. During the meeting of the First Continental Congress the delegates were entertained here by the City of Philadelphia and the Province of Pennsylvania at a magnificent banquet. On that occasion, the first toasts were dutifully raised to members of the British royal family; but—reflecting the temper of the times—the first of many toasts which followed was proposed to "Perpetual Union to the Colonies."

Today's visitors to the 100-foot Long Room hear background music played on a colonial harpsichord.

Au cours du premier Congrès continental la ville de Philadelphie et la province de Pennsylvanie offrirent aux délégués un magnifique banquet dans la grande galerie du premier étage du Palais du gouvernement. Aujourd'hui, les visiteurs sont accueillis dans cette salle au son d'une musique exécutée sur un clavecin d'époque coloniale.

Während des ersten Kontinentalkongresses wurde den Abgeordneten zu Ehren von der Stadt Philadelphia und der Provinz Pennsylvania ein grosses Festessen in diesem Long Room im ersten Stock des State House abgehalten. Der heutige Besucher des Saales hört im Hintergrund Cembalomusik aus der Kolonialzeit.

Durante la celebración del Primer Congreso Continental, la ciudad de Filadelfia y la provincia de Pensilvania ofrecieron a los diputados un magnífico banquete, que tuvo lugar en esta sala (Long Room) en el segundo piso de la State House. Los turistas que actualmente visitan esta sala pueden oír música de fondo ejecutada en un clavicordio colonial.

The Second Continental Congress also met in Philadelphia, convening on May 10, 1775—this time in the Pennsylvania State House. The fighting at Lexington and Concord had occurred the month before and the "redress of grievances" desired by the First Congress had not been obtained. The delegates provided for a Continental army and designated the Colonel from Virginia, George Washington, as General and Commander-in-Chief. Later in the year, the Navy was established and ships provided for.

The Second Congress met throughout the winter in the large Assembly Room of the State House with John Hancock serving as President. Sentiment for a complete break with Great Britain mounted continuously; and on June 7, 1776, the Virginia delegate Richard Henry Lee offered his resolution "that these United colonies are, and of right ought to be, free and independent States."

Lee's resolution was passed on July 2. While it was under consideration, Thomas Jefferson drafted the Declaration of Independence—intended to justify to the world the passage of the Lee resolution. After considerable amendment, Congress adopted the Declaration late in the afternoon of Thursday, July 4.

The Declaration was not signed that day. Congress merely ordered that the revised text be printed, and then turned to other business. Next day Congress resolved that the Declaration "be proclaimed in each of the United States, and at the Head of the Army." On July 19, it was ordered that the Declaration "be fairly engrossed on parchment . . . and that the same, when engrossed, be signed by every member of Congress."

The formal signing took place on August 2, 1776.

Le second Congrès continental se tint à Philadelphie en mai 1775 dans la salle de réunion du Palais du gouvernement de Pennsylvanie. Des combats avaient déjà eu lieu à Lexington et à Concord dans le Massachusetts. Le Congrès décida de créer l'armée continentale et lui donna pour commandant en chef un des délégués de Virginie : George Washington.

Le 7 juin 1776, un autre délégué de Virginie, Richard Henry Lee, déposa une résolution indiquant : ". . . que ces colonies Unies sont, et de droit devraient être, des Etats libres et indépendants." Le Congrès l'adopta le 2 juillet et pour justifier cette action au yeux du monde, on demanda à Thomas Jefferson de rédiger la "Déclaration de l'Indépendance". Elle fut adoptée le 4 juillet, non sans avoir subi de nombreux remaniements. Toutefois, ce n'est que le 2 août que la "Déclaration", une fois couchée sur parchemin, fut ratifiée par les membres du Congrès qui y apposèrent leur signature.

Der zweite Kontinentalkongress fand im Mai 1775 statt und tagte in der Versammlungshalle des Pennsylvania State House. Damals wurde bereits bei Lexington und Concord in Massachusetts gekämpft. Der Kongress organisierte die Kontinentalarmee mit George Washington, einem Abgeordneten aus Virginia, als Oberbefehlshaber.

Am. 7. Juni 1776 verfasste Richard Henry Lee, ein anderer Abgeordneter aus Virginia, eine Resolution, die besagte, "dass diese Vereinigten Kolonien frei sind und rechtmässig gesehen, freie und unabhängige Staaten sein müssen." Der Kongress nahm am 2. Juli die Resolution an, und um diese Handlung der Welt gegenüber zu rechtfertigen, wurde Thomas Jefferson beauftragt, den ersten Entwurf der Unabhängigkeitserklärung zu verfassen. Dieses Dokument wurde am 4. Juli mit verschiedenen Änderungen angenommen, aber erst am 2. August 1776 als Urkunde von den Kongressmitgliedern offiziell unterzeichnet.

En mayo de 1775 se reunió en Filadelfia el Segundo Congreso Continental y se celebró la sesión en la sala de reuniones de la State House de Pensilvania. Ya se habían librado combates en Lexington y Concord, en Massachusetts. Por tal motivo el Congreso organizó el Ejército Continental y nombró a George Washington, diputado de Virginia, Comandante en Jefe.

El 7 de junio de 1776, otro diputado de Virginia, Richard Henry Lee, presentó una resolución en la que se formulaba que "estas colonias unidas son y por derecho deberán ser estados libres e independientes". El 2 de julio del mismo año el Congreso adoptó dicha resolución. Con objeto de justificar esa acción ante el mundo, Thomas Jefferson fue designado para redactar la Declaración de Independencia. Después de considerables enmiendas, el 4 de julio se aprobó la Declaración "primorosamente copiada en pergamino", pero hasta el 2 de agosto de 1776 no fue firmada oficialmente por los miembros del Congreso.

Dear Larry & Andi,

Again, many thanks for your warm hospitality in Eugene. Please plan on giving us a chance to reciprocate in Philadelphia this Spring.

Best to you all,

Mike

MICHAEL H. KEAN, PH.D. / 264 FORREST ROAD / MERION STATION, PA. 19066

In CONGRESS, July 4, 1776.

The unanimous Declaration of the thirteen united States of America.

and our sacred Honor

Button Gwinnett
Lyman Hall
Geo Walton.

Wm Hooper
Joseph Hewes,
John Penn

Samuel Chase
Wm Paca
Thos Stone
Charles Carroll of Carrollton

Edward Rutledge.

Thos Heyward Junr.
Thomas Lynch Junr.
Arthur Middleton

George Wythe
Richard Henry Lee
Th Jefferson
Benja Harrison
Thos Nelson jr.
Francis Lightfoot Lee

John Hancock

Rob Morris
Benjamin Rush
Benja Franklin
John Morton
Geo Clymer
Jas Smith
Geo Taylor
James Wilson
Geo Ross
Cæsar Rodney
Geo Read
Tho M:Kean

Geo Read
Chas Livingston
Saml Lewis
Lewis Morris

Richd Stockton
Jno Witherspoon
Fras Hopkinson
John Hart
Abra Clark

Josiah Bartlett
Wm Whipple
Saml Adams
John Adams
Robt Treat Paine
Elbridge Gerry
Step Hopkins
William Ellery
Roger Sherman
Saml Huntington
Wm Williams
Oliver Wolcott
Matthew Thornton

There was no public celebration of the first Fourth of July. The text of the Declaration was published in Philadelphia newspapers over the weekend, and the entire document was publicly read in the State House yard at noon on Monday, July 8, 1776. Not until then did the great bell in the tower ring out its message of freedom. The bell had no crack at that time. Its inscription: "Proclaim Liberty throughout all the land . . ." had been placed on the bell more than twenty years before.

Il n'y eut pas de célébration publique le 4 juillet 1776. La "Déclaration" fut imprimée pendant le week-end et fut lue publiquement dans la cour du Palais du gouvernement le 8 juillet, à midi. Ce ne fut qu'à ce moment-là que la grande cloche, encore intacte, de la tour sonna son message de liberté. Et pourtant l'inscription : ". . . carillonnerez la liberté . . ." y figurait depuis plus de vingt ans.

Keine öffentliche Feier wurde am 4. Juli 1776 abgehalten. Die über das Wochenende gedruckte Unabhängigkeitserklärung wurde am Montag, dem 8. Juli bei einer Versammlung im Hofe des State House verlesen. Erst dann läutete die grosse Turmglocke ihre Freiheitskunde. Die Inschrift: "Verkündet Freiheit im ganzen Lande!" stand schon seit zwanzig Jahren auf dieser Glocke.

No se realizó ninguna celebración pública el 4 de julio de 1776. Durante el fin de semana se publicó la Declaración, que luego fue leída en público en una asamblea reunida, el lunes, 8 de julio, en el patio de la State House. En ese momento, desde la torre se oyó la gran campana tañer su mensaje de libertad. Desde hacía más de veinte años la campana llevaba grabada la siguiente inscripción: "Proclamaréis la libertad en toda la tierra para todos sus habitantes".

Congress resolved on June 14, 1777, "that the Flag of the United States be thirteen stripes alternate red and white; that the Union be thirteen stars white in a blue field, representing a new constellation." A Philadelphia seamstress, Mrs. Elizabeth Ross, made flags at that time for the government of Pennsylvania. One of the most popular stories of American history is that she cut a star with one snip of her scissors and sewed the first national emblem. A tiny house on Arch Street near Third is the Betsy Ross House and "The Birthplace of Old Glory."

Le 14 juin 1777, le Congrès décida que le drapeau des Etats-Unis serait composé de treize bandes alternées rouges et blanches et de treize étoiles blanches représentant l'Union. C'est Mme Elizabeth Ross, une couturière, qui cousit le premier drapeau dans la petite maison d'Arch Street connue depuis comme le "Berceau de la bannière étoilée (Old Glory)".

Der Kongress nahm am 14. Juni 1777 den "Stars and Stripes"—Entwurf für die Fahne der Vereinigten Staaten an. Elizabeth Ross, Schneiderin aus Philadelphia, nähte eine Fahne für die damalige Regierung von Pennsylvania. Die Entstehungsgeschichte der ersten Fahne machte das kleine Haus in der Archstrasse in der Nähe der Thirdstrasse als das Geburtshaus der "Old Glory" berühmt.

El 14 de junio de 1777 el Congreso resolvió que "la bandera de los Estados Unidos llevara trece rayas alternas en rojo y blanco, y que trece estrellas blancas sobre un fondo azul representaran a la Unión como una nueva constelación. La Sra. Elizabeth Ross, costurera de Filadelfia, en esa época confeccionaba banderas para el Gobierno de Pensilvania. Una modesta vivienda, situada en la calle Arch y la Third, es conocida como la Casa de Betsy Ross y "la cuna de la Bandera Nacional".

Six months after the Declaration, the cause of Independence seemed lost. The Continental Army had been defeated in New York and New Jersey and had retreated into Pennsylvania. Congress, fearing capture, had fled Philadelphia. Then General Washington turned the course of the war around by his bold stroke on Christmas night 1776. He recrossed the Delaware River from Pennsylvania to New Jersey, and routed the surprised Hessian mercenaries at Trenton and Princeton.

Two towns, one on each side of the river, are now called Washington Crossing. A state park preserves the historic ground, and every Christmas day men in colonial uniforms re-enact the icy crossing.

The following year, the British General Howe captured Philadelphia from the south after defeating the Continentals at Brandywine Creek. Howe occupied Philadelphia on September 27, 1777; and a week later, Washington attempted another surprise by marching on the city by way of Germantown. This failed, however, and his army went into winter quarters at Valley Forge.

The Battle of Germantown raged around Cliveden, the stone house of Justice Benjamin Chew. It still bears the marks of heavy cannonading.

En décembre 1776, la cause de l'indépendance semblait perdue mais le Général Washington changea le cours de la guerre par sa traversée inopinée du fleuve Delaware la nuit de Noël. Il mit l'ennemi en déroute et son armée eut le temps de se regrouper. Tous les ans le jour de Noël a lieu la reconstitution de cette traversée historique. L'année suivante, après que Philadelphie eut été occupée par les Anglais, Washington tenta une attaque imprévue de Germantown, mais ce fut un échec. La bataille fit rage autour de "Cliveden", la maison des Chew, qui porte encore les traces de la cannonade.

Im Dezember 1776 schien die Unabhängigkeitsbewegung verloren zu sein. Aber General Washington änderte am Weihnachtsabend den Kriegsverlauf durch seine unerwartete Überfahrt über den Delaware. Er besiegte den Feind bei Trenton und Princeton, und gab damit seinen Truppen die Möglichkeit, sich aufs neue zu gruppieren. Diese historische Überfahrt über den Delaware wird jeden Weihnachtstag wiederholt. Im folgenden Jahr, nachdem Philadelphia von den Engländern besetzt worden war, machte Washington noch einen Überraschungsangriff auf Germantown, aber diese Taktik misslang. Das Steinblockhaus der Familie Chew in Cliveden zeigt heute noch Spuren der Kanonade des Kampfes um Germantown.

En diciembre de 1776, la causa de la Independencia parecía perdida, pero el General Washington cambió el rumbo de la guerra al cruzar inesperadamente el río Delaware la noche de Navidad. Con esta maniobra confundió al enemigo y su ejército tuvo tiempo para reagruparse. Este cruce histórico es representado anualmente en dicho río en el día de Navidad. El año siguiente, después de que Filadelfia fue ocupada por los ingleses, Washington intentó otro ataque inesperado en Germantown, pero fracasó el esfuerzo. La casa de piedra Chew, llamada Cliveden, todavía ostenta las señales de los cañonazos durante la Batálla de Germantown.

The winter of 1777-78 was just beginning when Washington's army arrived at Valley Forge, about 20 miles northwest of Philadelphia. At first his soldiers endured unbelievable hardships while the camp was being organized and huts built for living quarters. Only General Washington's character and determination held the army together until supplies of food and clothing could be obtained.

Although the British in Philadelphia greatly outnumbered the troops with Washington, no serious effort was made to attack. On the contrary, the British found many friends and genial Tory hosts in Philadelphia and eventually settled into a busy winter round of dinners, dances and theatre parties.

Woodford Mansion, owned at that time by David Franks, agent of the Crown, was the scene of frequent entertainment. One of Frank's daughters married a British officer and General Howe was said to have been a regular visitor.

L'hiver 1777-78 venait à peine de commencer quand Washington vint établir son camp à Valley Forge, à une trentaine de kilomètres de Philadelphie. Les troupes en haillons et affamées eurent à souffrir de grands maux avant d'être ravitaillées et que leur camp soit organisé. Les Anglais, de leur côté, passèrent un hiver confortable dans la ville, reçus qu'ils étaient chez les sympathisants Tories et à Woodford.

Der Winter hatte gerade begonnen, als Washingtons Armee ins Winterlager bei Valley Forge, 20 Meilen von Philadelphia entfernt, einzog. Die zerlumpten und hungrigen Soldaten litten unglaubliche Not, bis Proviant erhalten und ein Lager aufgeschlagen werden konnte. Zur gleichen Zeit wurden die englischen Offiziere und Soldaten in der Stadt in den Häusern von Tory-Freunden und oft im Woodford Mansion bewirtet.

Al comenzar el invierno, el ejército de Washington acampó en Valley Forge a unas veinte millas de Filadelfia. Antes de poderse abastecer y organizar el campamento, las tropas andrajosas y hambrientas sufrían increíbles penurias. Mientras tanto, los oficiales y civiles ingleses pasaban una temporada agradable en la ciudad, constantemente homenajeados por los partidarios de los conservadores (Tory), y a menudo invitados a la mansión de los Woodford.

The rolling countryside of Valley Forge is beautiful in mild weather; and by the time the spring of 1778 arrived, the condition of Washington's army had greatly improved. The men were better housed, better fed and better clothed. Then, the spirits of all were lifted by news of the French Alliance which Benjamin Franklin had negotiated in Paris. The Commander ordered an entire day of Thanksgiving and celebration at Valley Forge—there were prayer services, enthusiastic marches on the parade ground and the sound of musket fire echoing through the hills at night.

In Philadelphia, news of French aid for the cause of Independence led General Howe at once to begin planning evacuation of the city. He remembered the year before.

When the British first took Philadelphia, their supply situation had been desperate. Washington's army cut off land routes, and British naval units were unable to penetrate the defenses of the Delaware River. It took nearly a week of intense bombardment of tiny Fort Mifflin, just below Philadelphia, before the river was opened. The heroics of Continental soldiers during that siege are regularly re-enacted at Fort Mifflin today.

Avec l'arrivée du printemps s'améliora le sort de l'armée de Washington à Valley Forge. On apprit la nouvelle de l'alliance avec la France et le moral remonta. A Philadelphie les Anglais firent immédiatement des plans pour évacuer la ville.

Als es Frühling in Valley Forge wurde, verbesserte sich die Lage von Washingtons Armee. Die Nachricht über das Bündnis mit Frankreich erreichte sie und stärkte den Mut der Soldaten. In Philadelphia machten die Engländer Pläne die Stadt unverzüglich zu räumen.

Cuando llegó la primavera a Valley Forge, mejoró la situación del ejército de Washington. Llegaron noticias de una alianza con Francia y los ánimos se elevaron. En Filadelfia, los ingleses de inmediato procedieron a hacer planes para evacuar la ciudad.

The British withdrew from Philadelphia in June 1778. Congress promptly returned, and on July 9, eight states signed the new Articles of Confederation. Most of the war thereafter was fought in the South, and it came to an end at Yorktown in 1781. In Washington Square in Philadelphia, the tomb of an unknown soldier of the Continental Army is a memorial to all who gave their lives for Independence.

After the fighting ended, a number of Quakers who had supported the Revolutionary cause and had been disowned by their own meetings for doing so, established the Free Quaker Meeting and built this attractive little meeting house at Fifth and Arch Streets. The Meeting is no longer active and the building is now part of Independence Mall.

The date stone on the north wall of the Free Quaker Meeting House testifies to the uncertainty of the times about government under the Articles of Confederation. Beginning with 1776, the author of the inscription calculated 1783 to be the eighth year "of the Empire."

C'est la bataille de Yorktown qui mit fin à la Guerre d'Indépendance. A Philadelphie, au Square Washington, on peut voir le tombeau d'un soldat inconnu commémorant le sacrifice de tous ceux qui sont tombés pour la nation naissante.

Les combats terminés, un certain nombre de Quakers qui, pour avoir soutenu la cause révolutionnaire, furent exclus de leur communauté fondèrent celle des Quakers Libres et firent bâtir leur propre temple à l'angle de la 5ème rue et d'Arch Street. Il est maintenant désaffecté.

Der Unabhängigkeitskrieg endete 1781 bei Yorktown. Das Grab eines Unbekannten Soldaten der Kontinental-Armee auf dem Washington Square in Philadelphia ist ein Denkmal zu Ehren aller, die ihr Leben für die junge Nation liessen.

Als der Krieg zuende war, gründeten die Quäker von Philadelphia, die aus dem Quäkerbund wegen Unterstützung des Krieges ausgeschlossen worden waren, das Free Quaker Meeting und errichteten ein Meeting Haus an der Ecke der Fifth und der Arch Street. Es hat heute keine aktiven Mitglieder mehr.

La Guerra de Independencia finalizó en Yorktown en 1781. La tumba de un soldado continental desconocido, situada en la Plaza Washington, en Filadelfia, constituye un monumento conmemorativo a todos los que dieron su vida por la joven nación.

Una vez terminada la guerra, los cuáqueros de Filadelfia, cuyos servicios religiosos habían sido prohibidos por haber apoyado a la guerra, organizaron la Asamblea de Cuáqueros Libres y construyeron un templo en las calles Fifth y Arch, donde ya no se celebran más servicios.

Delegates from the several states (no longer colonies) came back to Philadelphia on May 25, 1787 for a Convention called to revise the inadequate Articles of Confederation. They ended by drawing up a whole new frame of government—the Constitution of the United States.

The Convention gathered in the Assembly Room where the Declaration of Independence had been adopted eleven years before, and George Washington was chosen to preside. All through a hot, humid summer he guided the long and difficult debates, trying to find compromises which would unite the northern states and the southern states, the large states and the small ones.

The task was completed and the Constitution approved by the Convention on September 17, 1787. Pennsylvania's aged delegate Benjamin Franklin called attention to the carving on the back of Washington's chair. "Now at length," said he, "I have the happiness to know that it is a rising and not a setting sun."

We the People of the United... insure domestic Tranquility, provide for the common defence, promote the... and our Posterity, do ordain and establish this Constitution for the United...

Article. I.

Section. 1. All legislative Powers herein granted shall be vested in a Co... of Representatives.

Section. 2. The House of Representatives shall be composed of Members... in each State shall have the Qualifications requisite for Electors of the most numerous...

No Person shall be a Representative who shall not have attained to the... and who shall not, when elected, be an Inhabitant of that State in which he shall be...

Representatives and direct Taxes shall be apportioned among the several Sta... Numbers, which shall be determined by adding to the whole Number of free Persons...

Les délégués des Etats (non plus des colonies) revinrent à Philadelphie en mai 1787 pour la Convention qui devait rédiger la Constitution des Etats-Unis. Celle-ci fut adoptée en septembre de la même année. Benjamin Franklin, montrant la sculpture au dossier du fauteuil du président de la Convention, George Washington, déclara qu'il était heureux de savoir enfin qu'elle représentait le lever du soleil et non son coucher.

Die Abgeordneten der Staaten (die jetzt keine Kolonien mehr waren) kamen im Jahre 1787 nach Philadelphia, um die Fassung der Vereinigten Staaten auszuarbeiten. Am 17. September 1787 wurde die Verfassung angenommen. Der Abgeordnete Benjamin Franklin erklärte, es bereite ihm Freude, endlich zu erfahren, dass der Holzschnitt an der Lehne des Stuhles des Vorsitzenden eine aufgehende und keine untergehende Sonne darstelle.

Los diputados de los estados (ya no colonias) regresaron a Filadelfia en 1787 a fin de asistir a la Convención donde se redactó la Constitución de los Estados Unidos de América, que fue ratificada el 17 de septiembre de 1787. El diputado Benjamín Franklin declaró que se alegraba de saber por fin que el diseño del respaldo de la silla del presidente de la asamblea representaba un sol naciente y no un sol poniente.

George Washington's Capital City

George Washington was inaugurated President, and the first Congress met in 1790 in New York City. Within a few months, it was decided that a new "Federal City" would be established on the Potomac between Maryland and Virginia, and that, while it was being built, Philadelphia would be the capital of the United States.

Fine quarters were available here. The City of Philadelphia had just completed two new buildings which extended the State House complex to the entire Chestnut Street block from Fifth to Sixth Streets as it is today. From 1790 until 1800, the Supreme Court of the United States sat in the little building on the corner of Fifth Street which had been put up as a City Hall. The somewhat larger building at Sixth Street was turned over to Congress and has been known ever since as Congress Hall. The United States Senate sat in the ornate chamber on the second floor. Since three states were added to the original thirteen while the capital was here, the number of Senators' desks was increased to 32.

De 1790 à 1800, pendant la construction de la ville de Washington, Philadelphie fut la capitale des Etats-Unis. Elle venait juste d'ajouter deux bâtiments au Palais du gouvernement. Dans l'un de ceux-ci siégea la Cour suprême et dans l'autre, connu depuis sous le nom de Congress Hall, se tinrent les sessions du Sénat dans cette belle salle du premier étage.

Philadelphia war die Hauptstadt der Vereinigten Staaten von 1790 bis 1800, also zu der Zeit, als die Stadt Washington gebaut wurde. Die Stadt Philadelphia hatte dem State House gerade zwei neue Gebäude hinzugefügt. Eins davon diente als Sitz des Obersten Bundesgerichtes, das andere war die Kongresshalle. Der Senat der Vereinigten Staaten versammelte sich in dem prunkvollen Raum im ersten Stock.

Al paso que se erigía la ciudad de Washington, de 1790 a 1800, Filadelfia sirvió como capital de los Estados Unidos. La ciudad de Filadelfia acababa de agregar dos nuevos edificios al complejo de la State House. Uno de ellos sirvió de local a la Corte Suprema del país, y el otro se convirtió en la Cámara de Diputados, mientras que el Senado celebraba sus sesiones en la sala ornamentada en el segundo piso del edificio.

While Philadelphia was the capital, The United States House of Representatives met in the large ground-floor room of a building that had been intended as the county court house. This is where John Adams was inaugurated as the nation's second President in 1797.

An Italian sculptor, Giuseppe Ceracchi, came to Philadelphia in 1791 hoping to be selected to execute "A Monument Designed to Perpetuate the Memory of American Liberty." To demonstrate his skill, he presented to Congress a five-foot bust of *Minerva as the Patroness of American Liberty*. Congress did not authorize any monument at that time, but Ceracchi's first "Statue of Liberty" stood behind the Speaker's desk while Congress resided here.

A l'époque où Philadelphie était la capitale fédérale, la Chambre des Représentants siégeait dans la vaste salle du rez-de-chaussée du Congress Hall. Un grand buste de Minerve personnifiant la Liberté américaine fut offert au Congrès et placé derrière le fauteuil du président. C'est la première "statue de la Liberté".

Als Philadelphia die Bundeshauptstadt war, versammelten sich die Repräsentanten im grossen Raum im Erdgeschoss der Kongresshalle. Eine grosse Büste der Göttin Minerva, als der Schutzherrin der Freiheit Amerikas, wurde dem Kongress übergeben und hinter dem Schreibtisch des Vorsitzenden aufgestellt. Sie war die erste Freiheitsstatue.

Mientras Filadelfia era la capital federal, la Cámara de Representantes ocupaba la vasta sala de la planta baja de Congress Hall. Un gran busto de Minerva, Patrona de la Libertad Americana, fue presentado al Congreso y colocado en esta sala detrás del escritorio del Presidente de la Cámara. Se trataba de la primera "Estatua de la Libertad".

The Powel House, built in 1765 on Third Street near Spruce, was one of the finest houses in colonial Philadelphia. It was the home of Samuel Powel, a merchant who was also Mayor of the city in 1776. During the occupation of the city, it was used by the British High Commissioner. Later, when Philadelphia was the capital, George and Martha Washington were frequently guests here, and the Powels visited at Mount Vernon.

A much more modest house nearby at Fourth and Walnut was the home of the widow, Dolley Payne Todd. While Congress was in session in Philadelphia, one of the Virginia representatives, James Madison, asked to meet her. They were married in 1794. When Madison became President of the United States fifteen years later, Dolley Madison acquired fame as a White House hostess.

La maison de Samuel Powell, dans la 3ème rue près de Spruce Street, était une des plus belles de la Philadelphie de l'époque. Washington y fut souvent reçu. Dans une maison plus modeste, 4ème rue et Walnut Street, habitait une veuve, Dolley Payne Todd. Du temps où la Chambre siégeait à Philadelphie elle épousa un représentant de la Virginie, James Madison. En 1809, après l'élection de ce dernier à la présidence, elle se rendit célèbre par les réceptions qu'elle donnait à la Maison-Blanche.

Das Powel House in der Third Street in der Nähe der Spruce Street war eins der elegantesten Häuser des frühen Philadelphia. Als Washington Präsident war, weilte er hier oft zu Besuch. In einem bescheideneren Haus an der Ecke der Fourth und der Walnut Street lebte eine Witwe namens Dolley Payne Todd. Da der Kongress in der Nähe tagte, lernte sie den Abgeordneten James Madison aus Virginia kennen, den sie heiratete. Als Madison zum Präsidenten der Vereinigten Staaten gewählt wurde, wurde Dolley Madison als Gastgeberin des White House berühmt.

La Casa Powell, en la calle Third cerca de Spruce, fue una de las casas más elegantes de la Filadelfia de esa época. Durante su presidencia, Washington era visitante frecuente de la residencia. En una casa más modesta, en las calles Fourth y Walnut, vivía una viuda llamada Dolly Payne Todd. En la época en que el Congreso celebraba sus sesiones en las cercanías de su casa, uno de los representantes de Virginia, James Madison conoció a Dolly con la que contrajo matrimonio. Cuando Madison fue elegido Presidente de los Estados Unidos, Dolly Madison se convirtió en famosa anfitriona de la Casa Blanca.

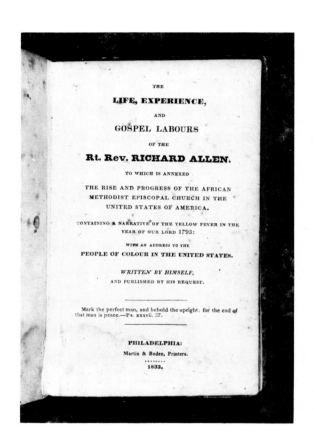

THE

LIFE, EXPERIENCE,

AND

GOSPEL LABOURS

OF THE

Rt. Rev. RICHARD ALLEN.

TO WHICH IS ANNEXED

THE RISE AND PROGRESS OF THE AFRICAN
METHODIST EPISCOPAL CHURCH IN THE
UNITED STATES OF AMERICA.

CONTAINING A NARRATIVE OF THE YELLOW FEVER IN THE
YEAR OF OUR LORD 1793:

WITH AN ADDRESS TO THE

PEOPLE OF COLOUR IN THE UNITED STATES.

WRITTEN BY HIMSELF,
AND PUBLISHED BY HIS REQUEST.

Mark the perfect man, and behold the upright: for the end of
that man is peace.—Ps. xxxvii. 37.

PHILADELPHIA:

Martin & Boden, Printers.

1833.

MOTHER BETHEL
AFRICAN METHODIST EPISCOPAL CHURCH
FOUNDED ON THIS SITE 1787
BY
RICHARD ALLEN
(A FORMER SLAVE)

THIS GROUND, PURCHASED BY RICHARD ALLEN
FOR A CHURCH, IS THE OLDEST PARCEL OF REAL
ESTATE OWNED CONTINUOUSLY BY NEGROES
IN THE UNITED STATES. THIS CONGREGATION
IS THE WORLD'S OLDEST AFRICAN METHODIST
EPISCOPAL CHURCH CONGREGATION.

• • •

THE FIRST CHURCH (1787) WAS AN ABANDONED
BLACKSMITH SHOP, HAULED TO THIS PLACE BY
THE TEAMS OF RICHARD ALLEN WHO WAS
ELECTED A BISHOP IN 1816.

•

"WE ALL WENT OUT OF THE CHURCH (OLD ST. GEORGE'S
METHODIST CHURCH) IN A BODY" AND "THEY WERE NO
MORE PLAGUED WITH US IN THEIR CHURCH."
RICHARD ALLEN

• • •

MAY OUR GOD CONTINUE TO BLESS MOTHER BETHEL AND ALL
HER CHILDREN, NOW SCATTERED THROUGHOUT THE WORLD,
BRINGING FAITH AND HOPE TO MILLIONS OF WEARY SOULS.

RING THE BELLS OF FREEDOM
THROUGHOUT THE WORLD
•
"RISE, SHINE, GIVE GOD THE GLORY
FOR THE YEAR OF JUBILEE."
OCTOBER 1961

Richard Allen, born a slave in Philadelphia in 1760, acquired an education, bought his freedom at age 17 and became both businessman and clergyman. He hauled salt for the Continental army and he belonged to historic St. George's Methodist Church where he regularly preached at the early morning service.

In 1787, when black worshippers at St. George's were directed to a segregated balcony, Allen and another minister, Absalom Jones, led a walkout from the church. They formed the Free African Society and conducted religious services in a rented storehouse. Absalom Jones united with the Church of England and founded St. Thomas African Protestant Episcopal Church. Its original building was near Fifth and Walnut Streets but St. Thomas is now located in West Philadelphia.

Richard Allen remained a Methodist. He bought an old frame shack which had been a blacksmith shop, hauled it to the lot he owned on Sixth Street near Lombard and made it the first home of Mother Bethel Church which occupies the same site.

Allen obtained a state charter for the independent church in 1796. Twenty years later, the first conference of the African Methodist Episcopal Church was held at Mother Bethel, and Richard Allen became the first bishop. He died in 1831, and is interred in the present church building. Congress has designated Mother Bethel as a national historical landmark.

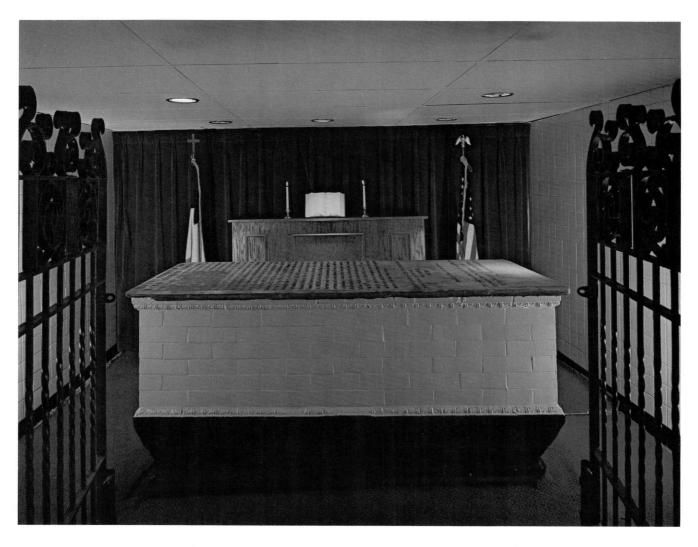

Richard Allen, ancien esclave, homme d'affaires et pasteur, acheta un terrain en 1787. Il y transporta une maison de forge abandonnée et y fonda Mother Bethel, église épiscopale méthodiste africaine. Il en devint le premier évèque et on peut y voir son tombeau. Cette église est classée monument historique.

Richard Allen, ehemaliger Sklave, Geschäftsmann, und Geistlicher schaffte sich im Jahre 1787 ein Grundstück an, brachte eine verlassene Schmiede an die Stelle und gründete Mother Bethel Church an der Sixthstrasse in der Nähe der Lombardstrasse. Er wurde zum ersten Bischof der African Methodist Episcopal Church. Seine Kirche steht immer noch auf demselben Platz. Richard Allens Grab ist in diesem Gebäude, das jetzt eine national-historische Erinnerungsstätte ist.

Richard Allen, antiguo esclavo, hombre de negocios y clérigo, compró un terreno en 1787, donde trasladó una vieja casa de madera—que en un tiempo había sido una herrería—y en ella estableció la iglesia de Mother Bethel en la calle Sixth, cerca de Lombard. Allen se convirtió en el primer obispo de la Iglesia Africana Metodista Episcopal, la cual está situada aún en el lugar original. La tumba de Richard Allen se encuentra en dicha iglesia y ha sido declarada monumento histórico nacional.

When a terrible plague of yellow fever swept Philadelphia in 1793, many government officials including President Washington fled the city. For a brief period that fall and again in 1794, a comfortable home at 5442 Germantown Avenue served as a temporary White House. With the Washingtons in residence, cabinet meetings were held here and the business of government was conducted in these rooms. Known as the Deshler-Morris House for two of its owners, the property is now in the care of Independence National Historical Park.

Early Philadelphia companies often held board meetings in the late afternoon and afterwards served dinner in lieu of paying fees to the directors. Such a dinner was in progress at the Mutual Assurance Company in December 1799 when news arrived of the death of George Washington at Mount Vernon. It was terminated at once in tribute to the great man so many directors had known personally.

The company's directors now meet monthly at its headquarters in historic Shippen-Wistar House at Fourth and Locust Streets and dine afterward in this beautiful old room. At the end of the meal, the dinner-jacketed directors rise, face the portrait on the east wall and adjourn with a toast "to the memory of General Washington."

Deux maisons évoquent le souvenir de George Washington. Celle des Deshler-Morris qui lui servit momentanément de résidence présidentielle en 1793 et celle des Shippen-Wistar où de nos jours ont lieu les dîners officiels d'une compagnie d'assurances qui se terminent toujours par un toast porté à la mémoire du Général.

Unter den verschiedenen Gebäuden, die die Erinnerung an George Washington wachhalten, befindet sich das Deshler-Morris House in Germantown, das 1793 als provisorisches White House diente. Ebenso erinnern die Dinner der Direktoren der Mutual Assurance Company mit ihrem traditionellen Toast an den ersten Präsidenten, an George Washington.

Entre los recuerdos que George Washington ha dejado en Filadelfia cabe mencionar la casa Deshler/Morris, en Germantown, que sirvió de Casa Blanca provisional en 1793. Asimismo, los banquetes que celebran los directores de la Mutual Assurance Company, que siempre terminan con un brindis tradicional en memoria del primer Presidente.

When the United States government moved to Washington, D.C., Congress presented Ceracchi's bust of Liberty to the Library Company of Philadelphia in appreciation for its service for over a quarter of a century. The Franklin-founded company had been quite literally the unofficial Library of Congress. It had been located on the second floor of Carpenters' Hall in 1774 while the First Continental Congress was meeting downstairs. Later, it served the Second Continental Congress as well; and after formation of the union, the Library Company was located in its own building just across Fifth Street from where Congress sat.

The first "Statue of Liberty" now occupies a place of honor in the present home of the Library Company at 1314 Locust Street. There, too, the very books, newspapers and handbills that were read by the first leaders of the United States are still available in the stacks.

In Carpenters' Hall, the second floor now houses the books of the Carpenters' Company itself. Some of the volumes date back to the Company's founding in 1724.

C'est au moment où se réunissait le premier Congrès continental au rez-de-chaussée du Carpenters' Hall que s'installait, au premier étage, la société d'achat de livres de Franklin. Cette dernière possède encore des journaux et des livres que lisaient les délégués. Quant à la corporation des charpentiers, certains livres de sa bibliothèque remontent à 1724, la date de sa fondation.

Als der erste Kontinentalkongress in der Carpenters' Hall tagte, befand sich die von Franklin gegründete Library Company im ersten Stock des Gebäudes. Bücher und Zeitungen aus damaliger Zeit befinden sich heute noch auf den Bücherregalen der Zentralstelle der Firma. Im ersten Stock der Carpenters' Hall findet man die Bücher der Firma Carpenters, die auf das Gründungsjahr 1724 zurückgehen.

Cuando el gobierno fue trasladado a Washington, D.C., el congreso obsequió el busto de la Libertad a la Library Company de Filadelfia. Actualmente la estatua se encuentra en el edificio de la firma en 1314 Locust St. Los libros y periódicos de la época todavía se conservan intactos en los estantes de la actual biblioteca de la firma.

A central Bank of the United States ("First Bank") was organized in 1791 under Alexander Hamilton, Washington's Secretary of the Treasury. It came to an end in 1811 when Congress refused to renew its charter, but the banking house remains on Third Street near Chestnut. Philadelphia's Stephen Girard bought the building and operated his own private bank there until his death.

Une Banque centrale des Etats-Unis fut fondée en 1791 sous la présidence de George Washington. Cette institution cessa d'exister vingt ans plus tard mais on peut toujours voir le bel édifice qui l'abritait dans la 3ème rue près de Chestnut Street.

Während Washingtons Amtszeit wurde eine zentrale Bank der Vereinigten Staaten gegründet. Seit 1811 existiert sie nicht mehr, aber das Bankgebäude in der Third Street in der Nähe der Chestnut Street ist heute noch eine der Sehenswürdigkeiten des Independence National Historical Park.

Durante la presidencia de Washington se estableció el banco central de los Estados Unidos. Aunque dejó de existir en 1811, su edificio, en la calle Third cerca de Chestnut, ha quedado como una de las atracciones del Independence National Historical Park.

Another of old Philadelphia's architectural gems is The Merchants' Exchange at Third and Walnut Streets, built in 1832. It became the first permanent home of the Philadelphia Stock Exchange. The Stock Exchange was founded in 1790, and its business was transacted originally in the city's coffee houses. The Merchants' Exchange building is now used for administrative offices of the National Park Service.

Un autre joyau architectural de la ville est l'ancienne Bourse, bâtie en 1832 au coin de la 3ème rue et de Walnut Street. Certains bureaux de l'administration des parcs nationaux y sont maintenant logés.

Die Kaufmannsbörse (Merchant's Exchange), an der Ecke der 3rd und der Walnut Street, erbaut im Jahre 1832, war das erste dauernde Heim der Börse von Philadelphia. Vorher waren seit ihrer Gründung im Jahre 1790 alle Verhandlungen in örtlichen Kaffeehäusern abgemacht worden. Die Kaufmannsbörse ist jetzt das Verwaltungsgebäude für die Nationale Parkbehörde.

El mercado de intercambio comercial (Merchant's Exchange), situado en las calles Third y Walnut y construido en 1832, fue el primer domicilio permanente de la Bolsa de Valores de Filadelfia. En la actualidad, este edificio aloja las oficinas administrativas del Servicio de Parques Nacionales.

Talented artists congregated in Philadelphia to earn their living doing portraits of leaders of the Revolution and of the Federal Government. One, Charles Willson Peale, began painting soldiers at Valley Forge and eventually filled a museum which he operated in the Long Room of Independence Hall for a quarter of a century. Peale was one of the founders of the Pennsylvania Academy of Fine Arts in 1805.

Some eighty of the Peale portraits and about one hundred others are now collected in a captivating Portrait Gallery maintained at Independence National Historical Park. Centerpiece of the exhibit is the historic wooden statue of George Washington originally carved for Independence Hall by William Rush.

The beautiful building which has become the permanent home of the Park's collection was built in 1819 for the Bank of the United States ("Second Bank") which Congress created in 1816. Located on Chestnut Street between Fourth and Fifth, this served as the Philadelphia Custom House for nearly a century after the Bank was terminated.

C'est le bel édifice construit pour la deuxième Banque des Etats-Unis en 1819 qui abrite aujourd'hui la collection de portraits de personnages célèbres de la Révolution et du gouvernement fédéral peints par des artistes de l'époque, en particulier Charles Peale. (Chestnut Street, entre la 4ème et la 5ème rue.)

Eine Gemäldegalerie des Befreiungskrieges mit einer Porträtsammlung der führenden Bundesbeamten, von zeitgenössischen Künstlern gemalt, wurde von den zuständigen Behörden des Independence National Historical Parks zusammengestellt. Sie befindet sich in einer Dauerausstellung in dem schönen Gebäude in der Chestnut Street zwischen der Fourth und Fifth Street, das ursprünglich 1819 als Bank der Vereinigten Staaten gebaut wurde.

El Independence National Historical Park ha coleccionado retratos de los primeros líderes de la guerra de la Revolución y del gobierno federal. Pintados por artistas de la época, los retratos se exhiben en un hermoso edificio en la calle Chestnut (entre las calles Fourth y Fifth), que fue construido originalmente en 1819 para el Banco de los Estados Unidos.

Philadelphia Today

Benjamin Franklin Parkway, a broad, tree-lined boulevard, sweeps directly from center city to the palatial Philadelphia Museum of Art on a hilltop at the entrance to Fairmount Park. Midway, the Parkway curves around a circular fountain at Logan Square. Near City Hall, it meets John F. Kennedy Plaza and the Tourist Information Center of the Philadelphia Convention and Visitors' Bureau.

De l'Hôtel de Ville, place John F. Kennedy où se trouve le centre touristique, l'avenue Benjamin Franklin conduit au Musée de Philadelphie et au Fairmount Park.

Der Benjamin Franklin Parkway erstreckt sich vom Stadtzentrum bis an das Philadelphia Kunstmuseum und den Fairmount Park. In der Nähe des Rathauses mündet der Parkway beim städtischen Verkehrsamt in den John F. Kennedy Platz.

La Benjamín Franklin Parkway se extiende majestuosamente en línea recta desde el centro de la ciudad hasta el Museo de Arte de Filadelfia y el Parque Fairmount. Cerca del Ayuntamiento se une con la Plaza John F. Kennedy y el Centro de Información Turística de la ciudad.

Philadelphia's monumental City Hall stands at the intersection of Broad Street and Market Street—the two main thoroughfares of Penn's original plan. It occupies a full city block, a massive structure of granite and marble, richly ornamented with architectural devices and more than 300 statues and carvings. The foundation walls which carry the stone building are over twenty feet thick. Workmen required more than twenty years to complete City Hall, including the tower topped by the founder's statue.

The unique stone stairways in City Hall include one in the south entrance which leaps upward two floors at a time. The ornate Mayor's Reception Room is the locale for ceremonies which range from press conferences to awards for police heroism. Near the top of City Hall tower is an observation platform for sightseers.

L'Hôtel de Ville est un édifice monumental de granite et de marbre à l'intersection des deux rues principales du plan de Penn. Il est orné de plus de trois cents statues et sculptures. La grande salle de réception sert de cadre à de nombreuses cérémonies municipales. Du haut de la tour on a une très belle vue sur la ville et les environs.

Das Rathaus von Philadelphia ist ein monumentaler Steinbau, der an der Kreuzung der beiden Hauptstrassen liegt, wie schon in Penns ursprünglichem Plan vermerkt wurde. Es ist durch übertrieben schwere Pracht gekennzeichnet, die aus über 300 Statuen und Schnitzwerken besteht. Das Empfangszimmer das Bürgermeisters wird für verschiedene städtische Veranstaltungen benutzt. Auf der Spitze des Rathausturms befindet sich eine Plattform, die dem Besucher eine Aussicht auf die Stadt bietet.

El Ayuntamiento de Filadelfia es una monumental estructura de piedra situada en la intersección de dos calles principales que fueron trazadas en el plano original de Penn. Dicho edificio está profusamente adornado con más de trescientas estatuas y esculturas. La Sala de Recepciones del Alcalde constituye el lugar donde se realiza toda clase de ceremonias municipales. Cerca de la cumbre de la torre del Ayuntamiento se encuentra un observatorio para los visitantes.

Around City Hall, directly below the Founder's statue, Philadelphia presents an outstanding demonstration of progressive mid-city urban renewal. Within a relatively few years, the entire heart of the city has taken on a new appearance. Penn Center and City Hall West Plaza have replaced the old Pennsylvania Railroad passenger station; the towers of Centre Square rise above the intricate dome of a lofty galleria; and in front of The Fidelity Mutual Life Building at Three Girard Plaza, the 28 foot Triune symbolizes in bronze the unity of people, industry and government in Penn's city.

En l'espace de peu d'années, le centre de Philadelphie a été transformé par la rénovation urbaine. Les tours jumelles de Centre Plaza dominent une galerie à toit ajouré et vitré. Plaza Girard, la sculpture monumentale en bronze de près de dix mètres de haut symbolise l'unité de la triade : l'homme, l'industrie et le gouvernement.

In verhältnismässig wenigen Jahren ist das Zentrum Philadelphias durch die moderne Stadtplanung verwandelt worden. Die Zwillingstürme am Center Square erheben sich über einer mit Glas überdachten Gallerie. Der Geist der Stadt wird symbolisiert durch eine 28 Fuss grosse Bronzestatue vor dem Fidelity Mutual Life Building.

En relativamente poco tiempo, el centro de Filadelfia ha sido transformado por la urbanización moderna. Las torres gemelas de Centre Square surgen por encima de una galería con una cúpula de vidrio. El espíritu de la ciudad está simbolizado por la Tríada de bronce—de 26 pies de altura—situada en frente del edificio Fidelity Mutual Life.

Philadelphia offers many reminders of Paris, among them these twin buildings at Logan Square, 19th Street and the Parkway, which are modeled after the Place de la Concorde. The one at the left is the Free Library of Philadelphia; the other houses the Municipal Court.

Ces deux édifices de Logan Square—la Bibliothèque municipale, à gauche et le Tribunal, à droite, sont imités de ceux de la Place de la Concorde à Paris.

Die Zwillingsgebäude am Logan Square, an der Kreuzung der Nineteenth Street und des Parkway, erinnern den Besucher an den Place de la Concorde in Paris. Das Gebäude links ist die Freie Bibliothek der Stadt Philadelphia; das andere ist das städtische Gerichtshaus.

Estos edificios gemelos en Logan Square, calle 19 y la Parkway, traen a la memoria la Place de la Concorde en París. A la izquierda se encuentra la biblioteca principal de Filadelfia, la "Free Library"; el otro es la sede de la Corte Municipal.

Stephen Girard, French merchant and banker, settled in Philadelphia in 1776. When he died in 1831, a widower without children, he left his large estate to the City to establish a residential school for young orphan boys. Called Girard College, it is located in North Philadelphia on what was one of his farms. Girard is interred here in Founder's Hall and the School is still maintained by his estate.

Stephen Girard, négociant et banquier français, qui vécut à Philadelphie de 1776 à sa mort en 1831, légua ses biens à la Ville pour la fondation d'un collège pour jeunes garçons orphelins qui porterait son nom. Girard est enterré dans le Founder's Hall que l'on voit ici.

Stephen Girard, ein französischer Kaufman und Bankier, der von 1776 bis 1831 in Philadelphia lebte, hinterliess sein grosses Vermögen der Stadt, um Girard College, eine Waisenschule für Knaben, zu gründen. Die Schule befindet sich dort, wo in der Vergangenheit seine Farm lag. Girard wurde in der Founder's Hall begraben.

Stephen Girard, comerciante y banquero francés, que vivió en Filadelfia de 1776 a 1831, legó su fortuna a la ciudad a fin de establecer Girard College, escuela para niños huérfanos que está situada en una de sus antiguas haciendas. Girard está sepultado aquí en el Founder's Hall.

The Philadelphia Museum of Art is a treasure house of masterpieces: a magnificent Greco-Roman temple crowning the hill and overlooking the downtown skyline, the Schuylkill and Fairmount Park.

This city-owned Museum contains ten acres of space, a hundred galleries and rooms, and more than 100,000 works of art. Along with outstanding painting and sculpture, it houses exhibits of tapestries, furniture, furnishings and fashions. Period rooms and architectural units have been assembled from many parts of the world, one of the most handsome being the Eighteenth-century drawing room from Lansdowne House, a fine townhouse in London's Berkeley Square.

Le Musée municipal des Beaux-Arts renferme de nombreux chefs-d'oeuvre de la peinture et de la sculpture de l'antiquité à nos jours. On peut y voir également des tapisseries, du mobilier et un musée du costume.

Das Kunstmuseum von Philadelphia beherbergt die Meisterwerke vieler Jahrhunderte. Es enthält hervorragende Gemälde und Skulpturen, Tapeten, Möbel, und Trachten aus vergangenen Zeiten.

El Museo de Arte de Filadelfia es un tesoro de obras maestras de todos los siglos. Además de las importantes obras de pintura y de escultura, posee colecciones the tapices, muebles y modas de diferentes épocas.

The Philadelphia Orchestra is admired and honored all over the world, but nowhere more than at home. In addition to its foreign travels and out-of-town engagements, the Orchestra plays about a hundred concerts each year to capacity audiences in its own beautiful hall, the Academy of Music at Broad and Locust Streets. The Academy was built in 1853, and is now the property of The Philadelphia Orchestra Association. The Orchestra was established in 1900.

L'Orchestre de Philadelphie est connu et estimé du monde entier mais nulle part ailleurs autant que chez lui. Il donne environ cent concerts annuels dans sa magnifique salle : l'Académie de Musique.

Das Philadelphia Orchestra hat Weltruf und ist auch zu Hause sehr beliebt. Jedes Jahr werden über einhundert gutbesuchte Konzerte in der schönen Halle der Academy of Music veranstaltet.

La Orquesta de Filadelfia es admirada y respetada en todo el mundo, pero nunca tanto como en su ciudad natal. Todos los años presenta más de cien conciertos, ante un numeroso público, en la Academy of Music, hermoso teatro que es propiedad de la Philadelphia Orchestra Association.

Subscription concerts are given at home by the Philadelphia Orchestra on Tuesday, Thursday, Friday and Saturday nights and on Friday afternoons. Philadelphians identify themselves to friends by the concert attended. From season to season they send in ticket orders early, hoping to acquire seniority in choice of seats. In summer, the Orchestra presents a five-week series of outdoor concerts at Robin Hood Dell in Fairmount Park. No admission is charged, and often the audience is as large as 30,000.

Des concerts d'abonnement de l'Orchestre de Philadelphie ont lieu à l'Académie de Musique les mardi, jeudi et samedi en soirée et le vendredi en matinée. En été, pendant cinq semaines, il donne des concerts en plein air auxquels assistent jusqu'à trente mille personnes. On reconnaît ici Eugene Ormandy.

Abonnementskonzerte werden von dem Philadelphia Orchestra jeden Dienstag-, Donnerstag-, und Samstagabend so wie Freitagnachmittag in der Academy of Music gegeben. Im Sommer gibt es eine Fünfwochenserie von Konzerten auf der Freilichtbühne des Robin Hood Dell im Fairmount Park. Oft werden einzelne Veranstaltungen von etwa 30 000 Menschen besucht.

La Orquesta de Filadelfia ofrece varios conciertos para sus subscriptores los días martes, jueves y sábados por la noche y los viernes de tarde, en la Academia de Música. En el verano también presenta una serie de conciertos al aire libre en Robin Hood Dell en Fairmount Park. Esta serie, que dura cinco semanas, atrae a más de 30,000 aficionados.

With forty accredited colleges and universities located in the city and suburbs, Philadelphia life is richly flavored with campus and classroom activity. Four medical schools are among the institutions here, three schools of law and schools of music, art, religion, business and science. Future doctors are changing classes at Thomas Jefferson University medical college; a Drexel University student rests in front of one of that school's new buildings; and University of Pennsylvania students cross a quadrangle.

Philadelphie et sa région comptent quarante "colleges" et universités comprenant quatre écoles de médecine, trois écoles de droit et des écoles de musique, de théologie, de commerce, de sciences et des beaux-arts.

Vierzig Colleges und Universitäten befinden sich in der Stadt und der Umgebung; unter ihnen sind vier Hochschulen für Medizin, drei für das Jurastudium wie auch Hochschulen für Musik, Kunst, Religion, Wirtschafts- und Naturwissenschaften.

Alrededor de cuarenta colegios y universidades acreditados están situados en Filadelfia, incluyendo cuatro facultades de medicina, tres de leyes, además de escuelas de música, arte, religión, comercio y ciencias.

Three colleges founded by the Quakers—Bryn Mawr, Haverford and Swarthmore—are located within a few miles of each other in Philadelphia suburban communities which carry their names. Haverford College was established in 1833 for men, and Bryn Mawr in 1880 for women. Swarthmore College was founded in 1864 and has always been co-educational. At Bryn Mawr, the English-style Martha Carey Thomas Building is named in honor of the remarkable woman who was the college's first dean and later its president. On the Swarthmore campus, a long walk beneath arching oak trees leads uphill to Parrish Hall, the main administration building.

Trois "colleges" fondés par les Quakers sont situés à quelques kilomètres les uns des autres dans la banlieue de Philadelphie : Bryn Mawr, Haverford et Swarthmore. Le premier est réservé aux jeunes filles, le second aux garçons et le troisième est mixte.

Drei Colleges—Bryn Mawr, Haverford und Swarthmore—wurden von den Quäkern gegründet. Sie liegen in der Philadelphia Vorstadt einige Meilen von einander entfernt. Bryn Mawr ist ein College für Studentinnen, Haverford für Studenten; Swarthmore wird von beiden besucht.

Tres universidades (colleges) fundadas por los cuáqueros—Bryn Mawr, Haverford y Swarthmore—se encuentran a pocas millas entre sí en las afueras de Filadelfia. Bryn Mawr es una universidad para damas; Haverford para hombres, y Swarthmore admite a ambos sexos.

Although Philadelphia is situated 90 miles from the ocean, it is one of the world's major seaports. The broad and deep Delaware River provides a safe and secure harbor, enabling seagoing vessels to come directly within the city's boundaries and dock within a mile of City Hall. The volume of shipping in and out of the Port of Philadelphia exceeds that of London.

Modern apartment towers now overlook Penn's Landing, the section of the waterfront where Penn and his Quaker settlers first came ashore.

Située à cent trente kilomètres de l'Océan, Philadelphie est un grand port fluvial sur le Delaware où peuvent accoster les navires de haute mer. L'endroit où a débarqué William Penn et ses compagnons, Penn's Landing, est maintenant dominé par de hauts immeubles modernes.

Obwohl Philadelphia 90 Meilen vom Ozean entfernt gelegen ist, hat die Stadt dennoch einen Hafen für Ozeandampfer, da der Delaware breit und tief genug ist, um den Schiffen die Einfahrt zu ermöglichen, so dass sie nur eine Meile vom Stadtzentrum entfernt anlegen können. Moderne Hochhäuser schauen auf das Hafenviertel herab, das "Penn's Landing" genannt wird.

Aunque Filadelfia está situada a 90 millas del océano, el ancho y profundo río Delaware provee un puerto seguro que facilita la entrada de los barcos de ultramar a los confines de la ciudad y muelles situados a una milla del Ayuntamiento. Las torres de modernos edificios de apartamentos dominan la zona portuaria, la que gracias a su historia es conocida como "Penn's Landing".

Because of its excellent port facilities, Philadelphia has attracted many diverse industries. Oil refining, chemical manufacturing and steel-making have all clustered nearby to take advantage of water transportation, and over the years, coal and grain have been important items of export through the port. Now, however, Philadelphia's waterfront bustles with another kind of activity—container shipping. Widespread truck transportation brings giant pre-packed containers the size of truck trailers directly to shipside. Giant cranes swing them into the hold or onto the deck of a container ship in minutes. Ship turn-around time is only a matter of a day or so.

L'expédition des marchandises par conteneur a causé une révolution dans le port de Philadelphie par l'emploi de plus en plus répandu des transports routiers. Les conteneurs sont acheminés directement à quai où, grâce à des grues géantes, le chargement des navires ne prend qu'un jour ou deux.

Der LKW-Transport hat den Hafenbetrieb revolutioniert und das sogennante "Container Shipping" eingeführt. Vorgepackte Kontainer, so gross wie ein LWK-Anhänger, werden an das Schiff gebracht. Innerhalb von Minuten heben riesige Kräne sie an Bord, und der Aufenthalt des Schiffes im Hafen wird dadurch auf einen Tag verkürzt.

La difusión del transporte por camión ha provocado un cambio total en las actividades portuarias de carga general en grandes recipientes. Estos enormes cajones, tan grandes como un camión de remolque, son trasladados directamente al propio muelle donde grúas gigantescas los embarcan en pocos minutos, reduciendo a un día el tiempo de rotación del barco.

Philadelphia's advantages as a port include the close and easy links between river, highway and rail transportation. Interstate Highway 95 (north and south) and the Pennsylvania Turnpike (east and west) are both at the doorstep of the waterfront and the vast industrial area of northeast Philadelphia.

Port activity extends well beyond the boundaries of the city itself. Nearby on the river are Camden, Trenton and Paulsboro, New Jersey; Chester and Marcus Hook, Pennsylvania; and Wilmington, Delaware. Shipping men call the entire area "Ameriport."

Le port de Philadelphie est étroitement raccordé aux voies de communication fluviales, routières et ferrées. Son activité s'étend de Trenton (New Jersey) à Wilmington (Delaware). Les sociétés de transport ont baptisé toute cette région : "Amériport".

In Philadelphia besteht eine enge Verbindung zwischen Fluss-, Strassen- und Bahntransport. Der Hafenverkehr erstreckt sich weit über die Grenzen der Stadt— von Trenton, New Jersey bis nach Wilmington, Delaware. Die Schiffer und Hafenarbeiter nennen die ganze Gegend "Ameriport."

Filadelfia dispone de fácil acceso y buenas conexiones de transporte por vía fluvial, carreteras y ferrocarril. Las actividades portuarias se extienden más allá de los límites de la ciudad—desde Trenton, Nueva Jersey, hasta Wilmington, Delaware. Los embarcadores denominan esta zona "Ameriport".

Philadelphia's big event on New Year's Day is the Mummers' Parade. Thousands take part in it, and hundreds of thousands come in family groups to watch. Since 1901, it has been a genuine folk festival, still entirely free of commercial floats and advertising.

The tradition is kept alive by scores of neighborhood clubs whose members devote much of the year to planning and working on theme ideas and costumes for the comic, fancy dress or string band divisions of the parade. On New Year's Day, Broad Street is closed to traffic. The parade begins at eight in the morning. It is usually well after dark before the last units reach the judges' stand at City Hall.

The string bands—unique Philadelphia organizations—are always the favorites in their elaborately feathered costumes. There is never a trumpet or a tuba. Banjos and violins are plentiful. And even in the coldest weather, many a sturdy Mummer walks five miles along Broad Street vigorously playing a bass fiddle strapped over his shoulder.

Une des traditions de Philadelphie est le défilé des "Mummers" (mascarade) le Jour de l'An. C'est un véritable festival folklorique qui n'est pas déparé par la publicité. Les différentes associations de la ville participent au défilé qui se déroule toute la journée. Parmi les plus appréciés sont les joueurs d'instruments à cordes qui sont propres à Philadelphie.

Eine Tradition Philadelphias ist die Neujahrsparade der sogennanten Mummer, ein wahres Volksfest, vollkommen frei von jeglichem Handelsgeist. Viele Tausend Mitglieder der verschiedenen Vereine der Umgebung marschieren mit; die Parade dauert den ganzen Tag. Philadelphias einzigartige Streichorchester sind sehr beliebt.

Una de las tradiciones más antiguas de Filadelfia es el desfile de enmascarados del día de Año Nuevo (Mummer's parade), auténtica fiesta folkórica sin ninguna publicidad comercial. Los clubes de barrio de la ciudad envian miles de participantes que desfilan durante todo el día. Las orquestas de cuerda de Filadelfia, únicas en su género, son siempre las favoritas del público.

Progress Plaza at Broad and Jefferson Streets is the prototype of minority-owned and minority-managed shopping centers rising throughout this country and abroad as ventures of Zion Investment Associates, founded by Dr. Leon H. Sullivan, pastor of Philadelphia's Zion Baptist Church. Members of his congregation pay $10 a month for 36 months to buy shares. They are aided by business and by the community.

Progress Plaza est un centre commercial constitué en société dont les actionnaires et les administrateurs appartiennent à des minorités. C'est le prototype de centaines de centres similaires aux Etats-Unis. Les membres d'une congrégation baptiste, Zion Baptist Church, fondatrice de cette société, payent dix dollars par mois pendant trois ans pour acheter des actions.

Progress Plaza gehört der schwarzen Minorität, die auch das Shopping Center verwaltet. Es ist ein Prototyp für ähnliche Zentren, die überall in den Vereinigten Staaten im Entstehen sind. Es gehört der Zion Investment Associates, die vom Pastor der Zion Baptist Church gegründet wurde. Die Geldmittel wurden von den Mitgliedern seiner Gemeinde so wie von Geschäftsleuten und der Bevölkerung des umliegenden Bezirks zur Verfügung gestellt.

Progress Plaza es un centro comercial cuyos dueños y directores representan un grupo de la minoría. Este es el prototipo de centros comerciales que se están estableciendo en los Estados Unidos. Los propietarios de este centro son los Zion Investment Associates, firma fundada por el pastor de la iglesia Zion Baptist y por los miembros de su congregación, cada uno de los cuales realizó una inversión de $10 mensuales por 36 meses para comprar las acciones.

An out of the ordinary shopping experience in downtown Philadelphia is a visit to the colorful sidewalk market on South Ninth Street.

Les étals en plein air des commerçants de la 9ème rue vous offriront un spectacle inhabituel à Philadelphie.

Ein interessantes Einkaufserlebnis in Philadelphia ist der Bürgersteigmarkt in der South Ninthstrasse.

Una experiencia interesante en el centro de la ciudad de Filadelfia es ir de compras al mercado al aire libre en la calle South Ninth.

Philadelphia's sports complex along South Broad Street is one of the best in the nation. The larger oval is Veterans' Stadium, home of the Phillies baseball team and the green-shirted Eagles of the National Football League. Just beyond is the Spectrum, the indoor arena where the Flyers play hockey and the Seventy-Sixers play basketball. Still further south is John F. Kennedy Stadium with a capacity of more than 100,000. This is where one of the country's major sports events, the Army-Navy football game, is played.

Dans la partie sud de Philadelphie se trouvent réunis ses trois plus grands parcs de sport. Le plus proche du centre est le Veterans' Stadium réservé aux matches de baseball et de football américain. Vient ensuite le Spectrum, stade couvert pour le basketball et le hockey. Plus loin encore, le John F. Kennedy Stadium qui a plus de cent mille places.

Die drei grossen städtischen Sportstadien liegen alle in South Philadelphia. Im Vordergrund befindet sich das Veterans' Stadium, wo Berufsspiele der Baseball- und Footballmanschaften stattfinden. Dahinter liegt das Spectrum, eine Hockey- und Basketballspielhalle. Im Hintergrund sieht man das John F. Kennedy Stadium, das über 100 000 Sitzplätze hat.

Los tres mayores centros deportivos de Filadelfia se encuentran agrupados en el sur de la ciudad. El más cercano es el Veterans' Stadium, que alberga los equipos profesionales de béisbol y fútbol. Cerca del anterior está el Spectrum, un estadio cerrado para hockey y baloncesto. Un poco más lejos se encuentra el John F. Kennedy Stadium, con capacidad para 100,000 espectadores sentados.

An unusual aspect of Philadelphia's remarkable renewal program is a requirement of the Redevelopment Authority that one percent of the cost of new construction projects be invested in works of art to be permanently displayed at the site. This is Bingham Court, Third and Spruce Streets, where new townhouses have been designed as links between rows of Eighteenth Century homes and high-rise apartments at the waterfront.

The sculpture, Unity, is by Philadelphia artist Richard Lieberman.

Ces maisons neuves de Bingham Court servent de lien entre celles du dix-huitième siècle et les grands immeubles modernes. Le plan de réaménagement prévoit qu'un pour cent du coût des immeubles neufs sera affecté à l'achat d'oeuvres d'art à ériger sur place.

La sculpture, l'Unité, est due au sculpteur Philadelphien Richard Lieberman.

Diese neuen Townhouses in Bingham Court sollen eine Verbindung zwischen den Häusern aus dem 18. Jahrhundert und den Hochhäusern herstellen. Ein Prozent der mit neuen Projekten verbundenen Kosten müssen in Kunstwerken investiert werden, die an dieser Stelle ihren Platz finden.

Die Skulptur, Einheit, ist das Werk des Künstlers Richard Lieberman aus Philadelphien.

Estas nuevas casas en Bingham Court fueron diseñadas a manera de transición entre las casas del siglo dieciocho y los modernos edificios de apartamentos de varios pisos. El uno por ciento del costo de los nuevos proyectos públicos de reconstrucción en Filadelfia debe ser invertido en obras de arte de exhibición permanente en el lugar.

La escultura, Unidad, es la obra del artista Richard Lieberman de Filadelfia.

At Christmastime, shoppers arrange their schedules to be at the John Wanamaker store at least once at show time. In the store's grand court, high above the large bronze eagle, which is Wanamaker's symbol, a holiday fantasy is presented with music, colored lights, and illuminated fountains.

On vient en foule assister au spectacle de Noël donné plusieurs fois par jour dans la cour principale du grand magasin "John Wanamaker".

In der Weihnachtszeit zieht die Weihnachtsvorstellung in der Haupthalle des Kaufhauses John Wanamaker viele Besucher mehrere Male am Tage an.

En la época de Navidad, la tienda John Wanamaker presenta espectáculos en su sala central, los que atraen multitudes varias veces al día.

"Faire Mount"-The Great Park

In 1682, the official surveyor preparing a plan of Philadelphia, designated a little hill on the east bank of the Schuylkill, "Faire Mount." William Penn originally intended to build his home there. Later, it was the site of the reservoir for the municipal waterworks. Today, the Philadelphia Museum of Art is located there. And beyond it, stretching for miles along both sides of the river, is Philadelphia's un-equalled, city-owned Fairmount Park.

The Park is within a few minutes walk or ride from residential neighborhoods on all sides and, by way of the Parkway, from the center of the downtown district. On summer week-ends and holidays, as many as half a million Philadelphians a day find open space, beauty, fresh air and recreation within its boundaries.

Sur un vieux plan de Philadelphie on a donné le nom de "Faire Mount" à une petite colline au coeur de la ville. Derrière, s'étend aujourd'hui le Fairmount Park de deux mille hectares. Aux beaux jours des centaines de milliers de personnes viennent y chercher l'air pur, la beauté et le délassement.

Auf einer frühen Karte von Philadelphia hatten die Landmesser einen kleinen Hügel "Faire Mount" genannt. Heute ist Fairmount der Name des grossangelegten Stadtparks, der sich über 4 000 Morgen Land durch die Stadt erstreckt. Im Sommer besuchen oft eine halbe Millionen Stadtbewöhner täglich diese Parkanlagen, wo sie die Weite, die Schönheiten der Natur, Spiele und sportliche Wettbewerbe geniessen.

Al levantar uno de los primeros planos de Filadelfia, el agrimensor bautizó una pequeña colina con el nombre de "Faire Mount". Hoy día, Fairmount es un parque municipal de 4,000 acres, que se extiende por el corazón de la ciudad. En los días estivales se puede ver hasta medio millón de personas gozando del aire libre, la hermosura y el recreo que ofrece este parque.

119

Games of rugby and cricket are played regularly in Fairmount Park along with baseball, football and soccer. Sailboats appear on the river almost the entire year around, and grassy banks provide a refuge for wildlife. Miles of trails are laid out for riding bicycles or horses, for jogging and for hiking; but of all park activities, perhaps family picnicking is the most popular.

The Philadelphia Zoo, the oldest in the nation and one of the best, has occupied a corner of the Park for a century.

Generations of Philadelphians have been proud of the Park, giving or bequeathing gardens, walkways, groves of trees and statuary to enhance it. One notable organization, The Fairmount Park Art Association, exists entirely for the purpose of providing works of art to decorate the Park.

Le Fairmount Park offre toutes sortes de distraction et aussi un refuge pour les oiseaux sauvages. On y trouve un beau jardin zoologique, le plus ancien du pays, un théatre de verdure et on peut y assister à des concerts en plein air. On peut faire de la voile presque toute l'année sur le Schuylkill.

Fairmount Park bietet den Stadtbewohnern viele Erholungsmöglichkeiten. Auch Wildvögel finden hier Schutz. Im Park befindet sich ein zoologischer Garten, ein Sommertheater und eine Freilichtbühne für musikalische Veranstaltungen. Boote sieht man auf dem Fluss fast das ganze Jahr über.

Fairmount Park ofrece varios tipos de entretenimiento a los habitantes de Filadelfia, así como un refugio para las aves silvestres. Asimismo comprende un excelente jardín zoológico, un teatro de verano y un auditorio al aire libre. Se pueden ver barcos navegando por el río durante casi todo el año.

"The Schuylkill Navy," based along Boathouse Row in Fairmount Park, is a long-established institution. Philadelphia oarsmen have won national and international honors over the years, and the Schuylkill course has been the scene of more championship rowing events than any other in the country.

Many high schools in the Philadelphia area have crews and participate in rowing races along with the colleges and universities. Even more active are the amateur clubs—women's and men's—whose members can be seen on the river in eights, fours, doubles and singles from early morning to near sundown in the summer season.

The banks of the Schuylkill take on a country fair atmosphere on regatta days when there are races sweeping down the river all day long.

Le Schuylkill a vu plus de courses d'aviron que toute autre rivière des Etats-Unis. Des régates y ont lieu où rivalisent les équipes des écoles de Philadelphie et des universités environnantes. Les jours de course ses rives prennent l'aspect d'une foire de campagne.

Auf dem Abschnitt des Schuylkills, der durch Fairmount Park fliesst, wurden mehr Ruderwettbewerbe veranstaltet als irgendwo anders im Land. Viele High Schools und Colleges aus Philadelphia und Umgebung haben ihre eigenen Ruderbootmanschaften, die an der Schuylkillregatta teilnehmen. Während dieser Tage herrscht an den Ufern des Flusses eine regelrechte Jahrmarktatmosphäre.

La pista de regatas del Schuylkill en Fairmount Park ha sido escenario del mayor número de campeonatos de remo que jamás se haya celebrado en ninguna otra ciudad del país. Gran cantidad de colegios y escuelas del área de Filadelfia disponen de tripulaciones que participan en las regatas del Schuylkill. En los días de regata las orillas del río se asemejan a una feria campestre.

The northernmost section of Fairmount Park branches from the Schuylkill and extends some five miles through the lovely valley of a creek with an Indian name, Wissahickon. Since William Penn's time, poets, painters and photographers have admired the natural beauty of the Wissahickon with its rushing water and rocky walls like a miniature canyon. Philadelphia bridge designers, with equal appreciation, have spanned the valley without spoiling its charm. Along much of the Wissahickon, automobiles are banned and the paths are reserved for walking.

Une des parties les plus agréables du Fairmount Park est la vallée d'un ruisseau au nom indien, le Wissahickon. La circulation automobile y est interdite et les sentiers sont réservés aux piétons.

Einer der schönsten Teile des Fairmount Parks ist das Tal, durch das ein Bach mit dem indianischen Namen Wissahickon fliesst. Dieses Tal ist teilweise für den Autoverkehr gesperrt; es gibt dort viele Pfade für Spaziergänger.

Una de las secciones más agradables de Fairmount Park es el valle que sigue el curso de un riachuelo que tiene el nombre indio de Wissahickon. Se prohibe el tránsito de automóviles a lo largo de las orillas del Wissahickon y las sendas están reservadas para los paseantes.

". . . This day my country was confirmed to me under the great seal of England," William Penn wrote on January 5, 1681, " 'Tis a clear and just thing, and my God that has given it me through many difficulties will, I believe, bless and make it the seed of a nation . . ."

Not quite a century later, the State House of Pennsylvania became the birthplace of the United States of America.

Le jour où le roi d'Angleterre lui fit don d'une province, William Penn écrivit qu'il pensait que Dieu en ferait le germe d'une nation. Moins d'un siècle plus tard le Palais du gouvernement de Pennsylvanie voyait la naissance des États-Unis d'Amérique.

An dem Tage, an dem William Penn diese Provinz als Geschenk vom britischen König erhielt, schrieb Penn, dass er glaube, sie werde einmal "das Saatkorn der Nation". Kaum ein Jahrhundert später wurde das State House von Pennsylvania die Geburtsstätte der Vereinigten Staaten von Amerika.

El día en que el rey británico le otorgó la provincia, William Penn escribió que la misma sería algún día "la semilla de la nación". Casi un siglo más tarde, la State House de Filadelfia se convirtió en la cuna de los Estados Unidos de América.